D1765713

Comhairle Contae Chorcaí
Cork County Council
LIBRARY SERVICE RULES

1. Readers must return this book on or before the last date shown below.
2. Books are loaned for 21 days and if kept beyond this time a fine will be charged.

www.corkcoco.ie/library

WRITING LIVES
Ethnographic Narratives

Series Editors:
Arthur P. Bochner and Carolyn Ellis
University of South Florida

Writing Lives: Ethnographic Narratives publishes narrative representations of qualitative research projects. The series editors seek manuscripts that blur the boundaries between humanities and social sciences. We encourage novel and evocative forms of expressing concrete lived experience, including autoethnographic, literary, poetic, artistic, visual, performative, critical, multi-voiced, conversational, and co-constructed representations. We are interested in ethnographic narratives that depict local stories; employ literary modes of scene setting, dialogue, character development, and unfolding action; and include the author's critical reflections on the research and writing process, such as research ethics, alternative modes of inquiry and representation, reflexivity, and evocative storytelling. Proposals and manuscripts should be directed to abochner@cas.usf.edu

Volumes in this series:

Erotic Mentoring: Women's Transformations in the University, Janice Hocker Rushing

Intimate Colonialism: Head, Heart, and Body in West African Development Work, Laurie L. Charlés

Last Writes: A Daybook for a Dying Friend, Laurel Richardson

A Trickster in Tweed: The Quest for Quality in a Faculty Life, Thomas F. Frentz

Guyana Diaries: Women's Lives Across Difference, Kimberly D. Nettles

Writing Qualitative Inquiry: Selves, Stories and the New Politics of Academic Success, H. L. Goodall, Jr.

Accidental Ethnography: An Inquiry into Family Secrecy, Christopher N. Poulos

Revision: Autoethnographic Reflections on Life and Work, Carolyn Ellis

Leaning: A Poetics of Personal Relations, Ronald J. Pelias

Narrating the Closet: An Autoethnography of Same-Sex Attraction, Tony E. Adams

LEANING

A Poetics of
Personal Relations

Ronald J. Pelias

Left
Coast
Press
Inc.

Left Coast Press Inc.

LEFT COAST PRESS, INC.
1630 North Main Street, #400
Walnut Creek, CA 94596
www.LCoastPress.com

Copyright © 2011 by Left Coast Press, Inc.

ISBN 978-1-59874-640-2 hardcover
ISBN 978-1-59874-641-9 paperback
eISBN 978-1-59874-642-6

Library of Congress Cataloging-in-Publication Data

Pelias, Ronald J.
    Leaning : a poetics of personal relations / Ronald J. Pelias.
        p. cm. — (Writing lives: ethnographic narratives)
    Includes bibliographical references and index.
    ISBN 978-1-59874-640-2 (hardcover : alk. paper) — ISBN 978-1-59874-641-9 (pbk. : alk. paper)
    1. Ethnology–Biographical methods. 2. Ethnology–Authorship. 3. Interpersonal relations. 4. Language and culture. 5. Communication and culture. I. Title.
    GN346.6.P45 2011
    302–dc22
                        2010053632

Printed in the United States of America

♾™ The paper used in this publication meets the minimum requirements of American National Standard for Information Sciences—Permanence of Paper for Printed Library Materials, ANSI/NISO Z39.48–1992.

Contents

For Mimi

Preface
Leaning *Into* a Beginning

Leaning: A Poetics of Personal Relations is a book about how bodies place themselves in relationship to other bodies. It works from a simple premise: in most cases, leaning toward others carries the greatest potential for meaningful and lasting relationships. Most often, "leaning toward" is how I want to be, although I do not always live up to my desire. When I lean in, I am an attentive, listening presence, trying my best to become attuned with another person. I want to gather, pull in, understand. I want that person to know that I am present, ready to engage, ready for what might be shared, ready for whatever sorrows or joys might come our way. I want to be a good reader of others, sensitive to what they might need, alive to what they are trying to say, open to what they may share.

Leaning toward, leaning in, calls for a negotiation of bodies. I find myself always asking how my body stands in relationship to another's. Simultaneously aware of my body and the other's, I watch the positioning, the resistance, the acceptance. I seek a comfortable fit, although I recognize that is not always possible or desired. When bodies tilt toward each other, they may begin to move in the same rhythm, with the same pulse. They may sense themselves in an empathic encounter, each understanding and feeling with the other. They may warm by the presence of the other. Sometimes, however, when they lean in, they discover differences, points of tension. They may struggle to find places of connection and agreement. They may become aware of the work that bending in requires; they may feel its pull, its weight. They may resent it. Yet, they often continue, particularly in long term relationships, because they sense its promise, trust in its possibilities. They want to remain leaning in. They know that when they slant in, they thrive in each other's sense of self and acknowledgment of the other. And when they are there, leaning in, present, they know they are participating in an ethic of care.

In not all situations, however, is leaning in the best stance to take in relationship to another. Sometimes, I lean away from others because I do not like who I become when I lean toward them. Perhaps I might find myself uncomfortably transformed, engaging in behaviors that I would rather not do, that I wish to resist. Perhaps I might assume a role (e.g., parental, passive-aggressive) I would rather not play. Whatever the case, when I lean in, I want to hold a positive sense of myself. If I don't, I want to pull away.

Sometimes, I may decide to not lean in because I am occupied with other concerns, because I recognize the impossibility of reaching toward all others, because I do not wish to expend the energy it takes. Not all circumstances demand, allow, or encourage leaning in. Sometimes I do not lean in because I sense my presence would not be welcomed. Thus, the choice is not always my own. I do know, however, that the decision to not embrace, whether mine or another's, can be hurtful. It can become a statement of value, a judgment, marking who does and who does not matter.

Sometimes I do not lean in because of cultural practices and habits. Where I've been told I should live limits the opportunities I have for interacting with others. Who I've been told I should or should not embrace limits who I do embrace, even when my desires might unfold differently. Cultural markers, such as class, race, gender, sexuality, and religion, encourage particular partnerings. I may lean in across these designations, but I am culturally aware of the risks. To the extent that I unreflectively adopt a culture's arrangements, when I fail to lean in because of how I am positioned, or when I hesitate in engaging others because of the potential dangers, I am lessened.

Sometimes I do not lean in because I stand in opposition to what the other represents. My sense of self is often formed in contrast. When differences become marked, I like myself best if I have first leaned in, tried to understand others in their intellectual and emotional complexity, tried to be open. Before turning away, I want to be the person who makes the effort, who reaches out, body slanting in. I want to forge common ground and mutual respect. I want to remember our humanness. I do not, however, always do what I should.

Instead, I find myself leaning with others who share my ways of seeing. Our bodies come together, form alliances. We lean together, focused upon the joys of our company and vigilant to the threats of those who may do us harm. Bonded, we settle together, armed with the strength of our commonality. In partnership, we resist those who might push us in directions we would rather not go. Leaning with others, then, becomes a personal comfort and a political force. Affinity breeds conviction, institutionalizes power. It comes with the risk of personal blinders and political indoctrination, of empty associations and hollow sloganeering. Yet, without leaning with others, we face isolation, struggle with the strength of our own thinking, accept the impossibility of change. We need to stand with others in kinship for our own and others' benefit. We need to lean together, bodies linked, for productive personal and cultural work. We need each other's presence, need the weight of others' bodies.

It comes as little surprise, then, that I find myself leaning on others. To stand, I may need help. To speak, I may need guidance. To be, I need love. I depend upon others for their support, their companionship, their acceptance, their love. I am sustained through interaction, made again and again, by the generosity of others. Living in a relationship marked with love, I feel most alive, most fully human. I need others, and I want others to need me, to lean on and with me, to find my body a place of trust and comfort, a place where love might flourish.

To do the leaning I wish to do in this book, I call upon a number of qualitative methods, including personal narrative, autoethnography, poetic inquiry and performative writing. These methods share much in common, making clear generic separation sometimes difficult. Yet each does seem to foreground certain dimensions.

The personal narratives are stories, told with the desire to make sense of individual experience, strive for a personal logic, search for an order that will hold still, but might best be seen as a momentary settling. Using personal narratives, I function, like the autobiographer and memoirist, by pulling the past forward, by working to collect images, fragments, and splinters into coherence, by peering into cracks and crevices, into dark shadows. I grapple with what memory hardens, with how archives hook, and with how history hides. I tell a story of a life, reaching, seeking scripts for an always more promising and ethical future. When I turn to a personal narrative, then, I am offering an individual account of human experience. My desire is to make sense of relational life, to demonstrate how I and others think, feel, and behave, and to offer alternative ways of being.

The autoethnographic pieces are writings designed to evoke my own experiences as a strategy for excavating culture. I am always culturally situated, always reflecting my positioning. As an autoethnographic writer, I speak as a participant caught in public logics and as a telling example, and, if sufficiently reflexive, as an error calling for change. Autoethnography, often pushing against culture's rules and regulations, positions me as cultural worker, as someone who refuses to accept practices that diminish and betray others and as someone who is willing to let his vulnerable self be used as a strategy for intervention. In my digging, in my correctives, I uncover alternatives for living, for being a better person. Calling upon autoethnographic methods, then, I work to investigate culture by reflecting upon my own situatedness as a cultural member or outsider.

The poetic pieces, broadly and narrowly conceived, are a means of inquiry. The turn to the poetic reflects my faith in language's evocative power, in its ability to capture more fully than any other representational mode the heart of human relationships. I rely upon its sensuous, figurative and expressive muscle. I want the poetic to shape random experience into form, to open what is closed, and to carry despite the unbearable weight. I want the poetic to discover how meaning feels and how feeling means. I want the poetic to show how ideas only matter when they attach to bodies, how bodies only thrive when both the heart and the head language and live in concert. From the poem to the evocative tale, the poetic allows me a deep entry into my interpersonal life, gives me explanations that seem the most fully rendered, the most telling, but still lets me recognize it as only a beginning:

Beyond

Poets live well beyond the decimal
point in pi. Instead of measuring
a circle, they write by rubbing
against what tries to contain.

It's been raining all morning and
I've made love with my wife.
It's too wet for the birds to visit
the feeder. I've started this poem.

Poetic inquiry, then, encourages me to deploy poetic devices to shape and evoke experience, to shun the prosaic for the poetic, to reach for the expressive.

The performative writing is a doing, sometimes conventional and sometimes disruptive, coming into being. Performative writing emerges as a generative opportunity and stands as a pedagogical lesson. Nervously, I accomplish what I say and, as I do so, I open material possibilities, options that I hope prove telling and seductive. I live in the subjunctive, the "as if," always wondering what utterances should be shared, always questioning the ethical consequences of my actions. I live ready to take away what I currently assert, knowing how assertions silence, how they privilege the present at the expense of the absent, how they limit by turning themselves into law. Yet, I assert, believing that each moment is a petition for action and a call that I cannot deny. I have no other choice than to put forward performances for consideration, than to take the stage as a cautious advocate, than to allow myself to be publicly exposed. As a performative writer, then, I remain aware that language has material consequences and that I must, with the performances I offer, work ethically as I strive for a better world.

This book is an invitation, as qualitative methods often are, to lean in, to witness one writer struggling to make sense of personal relationships. It is divided into five sections: "Languaging Relationships," "Listening to Myself and Others," "Watching Men," "Holding Friends and Lovers," and "Carrying Family." Each section offers several essays on their respective themes. None is exhaustive. They are perhaps best seen as tentative touches, attempts to make contact without wanting to be intrusive. The invitation allows for roaming, a leaning in here or there, in the hope that resonance or dissonance might bring our bodies into deeper connection. The invitation is open to the reader's leanings. I do, however, see some potential uses of the book that might prove productive.

First, the book might be read as a case study of a white, middle class, sixty-something, heterosexual, able-bodied man, culturally and

historically situated, who, based upon a lifetime of personal relationships, tries to make sense of it all. In this reading, the sections of the
book are best seen as a story, one of many that could be told, that pulls
together the relational issues I have found the most telling in my life. The
tale, as all stories are, is not only partial but also partisan, told from my
point of view. This story, then, is my attempt to establish some coherence
to experiences that resist easy and satisfying renderings. It stands as the
best and most honest effort I can currently offer, shared for personal and
scholarly use.

Second, the book might be seen in keeping with a typical course in
interpersonal communication. Organizationally, it follows a traditional
scheme common in interpersonal circles. The first section, "Languaging
Relationships," links personal relations to communication, to interaction based in talk between meaning-making and meaning-seeking
individuals. "Listening to Myself and Others," section 2, turns to listening as a productive strategy for coming to know others and oneself.
Understanding how perception, attribution, cognitive processing, identity, and self-conceptions come into play in personal relationships allows
for more meaningful contact with others. The third section, "Watching
Men," locates personal relations in gender and sexuality. "Holding
Friends and Lovers" and "Carrying Family," the fourth and fifth sections, work with intimate relationships, those of friends, partners, and
family members.

As it follows these familiar themes, it does not attempt to offer a
survey of relational literature; many other sources do this quite well.
Instead, it shows how one individual navigates, sometimes well and
sometimes not, with both heart and head through these areas. In this
sense, the book might function as a companion text to a more traditional text in interpersonal communication, or it might serve as a series of
examples for readers who wish to tell their own stories as a means for
making sense of their own personal relationships.

Third, the book might function as a series of methodological
exemplars. As noted, it relies on personal narratives, autoethnography,
poetic inquiry, and performative writing. Each of these methodological
strategies participates in a growing body of scholarly methods that fall

generally under the label qualitative inquiry. Each method has its advocates and its detractors. While I do not make an explicit case for any of these methods, my desire is to have each essay speak implicitly to the potential power. For better or worse, the argument on their behalf rides upon my use. In this way the book might serve as an illustration of qualitative methods in action, as examples that compliment detailed articulations of methodological assumptions and procedures.

I end this preface by leaning toward those who have made this project possible. First, I thank my writing group—Jonathan Wyatt, Ken Gale, Tami Spry and Larry Russell—who continue to teach me what it means to lean in and who are responsible for the birth of the leaning metaphor in my thinking. Second, I owe considerable gratitude to my wife, Mimi Hinchcliff-Pelias, who not only was supportive throughout the project and allowed herself to be written by my clumsy hand, but who also provided her keen editorial eye. Without her insights, the book would be significantly diminished. Third, I am grateful to Lesa Lockford, Lee Jenkins, Carolyn Ellis, Art Bochner, Bud Goodall, Norman Denzin, and Chris Poulos whose intelligence, passion, and spirit are with me on every page. Fourth, I offer my ongoing appreciation to my departmental colleagues at Southern Illinois University who challenge and inspire me everyday. Fifth, I thank Mitch Allen of Left Coast Press, Inc. for his support and assistance. The world is a better place because of the labor of Mitch Allen at Left Coast. I also appreciate the hard work of the Left Coast staff, particularly the considerable contributions of Michael and Hannah Jennings. Lastly, I acknowledge the following publishers for their permission to reproduce, some in revised form, the essays and poems listed below.

Essays

Elsevier, "Walking and Writing with Laurel Richardson: A Story in Poems," *Studies in Symbolic Interaction* 27 (2004), 41–54.

Routledge, "A Personal History of Lust on Bourbon Street," *Text and Performance Quarterly* 26 (2006): 47–56; and "Relational Language: A Poetic Sense-Making," under the title, "Imagining a Poetics of Communication," *Southern Communication Journal* 68 (Summer 2003): 335–45.

Sage, "Jarheads, Girly Men, and the Pleasures of Violence," *Qualitative Inquiry* 13 (October 2007): 945–959; and "Stories We Do and Do Not Tell" under the title, "H. L. Goodall's *A Need to Know* and the Stories We Tell Ourselves," *Qualitative Inquiry* 14 (October 2008): 1309–1313.

College of William and Mary, "Remains," under the title, "Remains: What Is Left, Kept, and Next," *Theatre Annual* 60 (2007): 23–31.

Left Coast, "Making My Masculine Body Behave," *International Review of Qualitative Research* 1 (May 2008): 65–74.

Poems

"The Relationship," *The Spoon River Quarterly* 4 (Spring 1979): 29–32.

"Once Upon a Romance" and "Prelude to a Contemporary Exit," *Vanderbilt Street Review* 4 (1983): 37, 140.

"In Search of a Love Poem," *13th Warrior Review* 4 (Fall 2001): np.

"Fragments of Intimacy" and "What Gets Left Behind," *Zillah* 2 (Spring 2002): 35.

"The Point of the Shovel," *Whetstone* 18 (2002): 30.

"Stone, Shell, Feather," *360 Degrees* (October 2003): 30–31.

Part 1

Languaging Relationships

I am drawn to language, to speech acts, to communicative exchanges as the most telling aspects of my personal relationships. I lean in through language; I distance myself through language; I negotiate meaning through language. In short, I language my way into being a social being. Constituted in interaction, I am formed by the language that passes between me and others. And I make sense of my relationships by finding language that provides some account of my personal observations and feelings. I share what I come to understand and, once again, find myself constituted by that sharing. Such a process leads me to begin this book by first looking at how language unfolds in my relationships, how speech acts become definitional, how communication establishes, for better or worse, my relationships with others. I stand in agreement with Stewart (2009) who argues that *"there's a direct link between the quality of your communication and the quality of your life"* (p. 6).

As I proceed, I reach for language that transcends the phatic, the everyday, a language that finds its way into the heart of a subject. In writing from and to the heart, I bring forward a self who wants to reveal his cognitive and affective sense-making. To do so, I rely on language's evocative and seductive power, its potential for creating new ways of seeing and feeling, its ability to construct a rendering that seems in the moment right. I work against the permanent, satisfied account. Instead, I seek a language that marks a place, a time, an unfolding.

Chapter 1, "Some Substantiated and Unsubstantiated Claims for Communication," establishes a beginning point as I consider my relationships with others. It offers a series of claims about communication that I see as fundamental to my everyday interactions. Chapter 2, "Relational Language: A Poetic Sense-Making," continues the exploration by identifying key communication dimensions that influence my engagement with others. "Struggling for Speech," the third chapter, describes several moments when I have felt speechless, rendered silent by what has been said to me. It functions not only to portray such moments but also to demonstrate how language lives as a limitation, an inadequacy. Chapter 4, "Relational Associations," maps how experience feeds into experience, how relational sense-making comes from an accumulation of linked interpersonal encounters, how memories trigger memories. In such a way, I form cognitive and affective structures for understanding. I *become* my way of processing. "Stephen Dunn and the Poetics of Living," the final chapter in this section, takes the work of Stephen Dunn as an example of how a poet's work might provide interpersonal insight, might serve as poetic inquiry. Dunn, a poet I much admire, writes me and my relationships. I use his poems, his carefully-wrought language, to show how it teaches me how I live my life with others.

My relational life is a story of language, of communication, told in the words that I can muster.

Chapter 1
Some Substantiated and Unsubstantiated Claims for Communication

My personal relationships are built through communicative acts, through the variety of ways in which talk ties me to or positions me away from others. I find my place in relationship to others through interaction, through language, through speech acts that do and do not mark connection. My words, for better and worse, locate me in relation to others. I write this piece as a series of substantiated and unsubstantiated probes, suggesting how communication pulls me into and pushes me away from others. I offer a series of claims about communication, some that would gather much agreement and others that might be met with some resistance. Following each claim, I show how it is indicative of my communicative practice, how it structures and defines my personal relationships.

Communication speaks lives into being.

> Born into language, into symbols, into iterations that I perpetuate, I communicate, meeting and engaging others who share the same system. I language along in my mother tongue: I think in English; I speak in English; I feel in English. I do not have command of any other system. I am an English speaking man who seeks English speaking others. It began with my mother's voice.

Communication agrees to be agreeable. It has no other choice. It lives for the interlocutors who know the rules.

When asked a question, I try to answer. When spoken to, I respond. When I discover myself within a form, I work for its completion. When a noun demands its verb or a verb its object, I offer it. When a clause or adverb has trouble finding its location, I help it find its way. When I use a given word or gesture, I believe I am using it in the way others might. In doing such things, I join a socially constructed world. I participate, as Pearce and Cronen (1980) suggest, in a "coordinated management of meaning." I like being a part of it, like that it allows me to interact with others, like that it defines me as cooperative, relatively competent, and, by some measures, sane.

Communication always needs someone, always is in search of an audience.

Without another, communication is nothing more than an echo chamber. I use communication, that "continuous, complex, collaborative process of verbal and nonverbal meaning-making" (Stewart, 2009, p. 16), to reach beyond myself, to reach into relationships. My speech always wants another's ear.

Communication is the distance between what is conceived and finally said and what is heard and ultimately received.

I am pulling together words, sentences, this beginning chapter. I want what I'm thinking and feeling to find its form, to be clear, understandable. I hope what I write is read, taken in, understood in a way that I intend. I know there is always slippage. I struggle to find you. I hope you will reciprocate. Meaning, the familiar phrase goes, is in people, not in words. I would add that meaning-making is what makes us people, not puppets.

Communication is a dance where the dancers are always learning the steps. Some are graceful; some are not.

Connected, I want a waltz of words, a ballet of breath, a tango of taking. I move for the right feel at the right time. Sometimes I stumble; sometimes I soar. Circling, bending in instead of away, and touching are the beginning steps. I applaud the generosity of assessments that forgives missteps. In doing so, one might find grace.

Communication moves among lives deciding where to place its affection.

For the most part, I like those who like me and dislike those who don't. I become uneasy when something feels unsettled. I seek balance (Festinger, 1957). I prefer the gentle rocking of a calm sea. I feel best in a relationship when I can reduce uncertainty. I work to earn trust. I hope that whatever I might disclose is secure, protected (Berger & Calabrese, 1975; Berger & Kellermann, 1994). I never want to feel alone, stranded on a rope bridge over a deep ravine. In some cases, my desire is to become close to another, to move beyond, penetrate barriers that might exist (Altman & Taylor, 1973). I might proceed with a surgeon's precision or I might carry on like a frightened soldier hiding behind a hill. I surprise and anger myself. I make attributions, sometimes based on what I consider internal or external causes and sometimes based on what I consider controllable and stable causes (Heider, 1958; Weiner, 1986). I am a biased judge. I place my affection where it feels safe.

Communication is always an act of confession. If nothing else, it confesses its desire to communicate.

When I speak, I name myself. I make present what I see as noteworthy, mark what I feel carries weight, establish what I think is of value. I share, and in doing so, I am social and socially constituted. And when I am fully there with someone, leaning in, I have my best chance of hearing, of opening, of connecting.

Communication is often a story that attempts to tame chaos.

I come to communication, cohabitating with compatible and incompatible claims, concerns, and conclusions. I search for tales that could be true, that settle, that bring order to my fragmented world. I am witness to it all, narrating, whenever possible, coherence out of chaos.

Communication happens by removing a finger from each ear, by shedding blindfolds, and by attending to communication's march.

My failures to communicate are often failures of generosity. Barriers to my communication efforts are best broken by throwing bricks at my own head. Conflict is a personal and interpersonal opportunity. Seldom do I rise to the occasion. Instead, I collapse under the clash, close off, circle myself in my own logic. I want exchange, give and take, pollination and honey. I seek rewards with minimal costs, a coordinated cadence.

Communication needs empathy as roots seek water.

I learn how to and how not to communicate by beginning and ending with the other. Empathy gives life, allows a taking in, a sense that entry is possible, nourishing. It permits me, at least to some degree, to understand and share another's feelings. And when I do empathize, I flourish.

Communication can mobilize immobility.

It lets me inch away from my own methods and mediocrity. With it, I can irritate the everyday. It allows me to offer a prayer on behalf of the possible.

Communication, at its best, is two "I's" leaning in.

Chapter 2
Relational Language
A Poetic Sense-Making

I want words to lay claim, to find the heart, to insist upon moving close. Instead of offering a study of relational dimensions in the variable analytic tradition, I excavate feelings I've had when engaging in relational talk. My aim is to capture my emotional sensibility linked to everyday understandings of relational issues. I strive to write communication's affect as I name dimensions that play upon my interactions with others. I work with poetic probes to circle the subject, to uncover what often remains unsaid. In this way, I offer one account of personal and interpersonal sense-making that may or may not find resonance for others.

Intentions

My intentions live in the belief that communication is possible. They are always reaching out, stretching to make some connection. But they are nothing more than the calling waves collapsing on a silent beach, nothing more than the wind meeting the resistant shore, nothing more than the drowning hand's best efforts. I do not count on them. In their aftermath, I often pull away, watch everything become caught in their current. Often, I cannot see anything. Intent is food for the sharks.

Fictive data:

"You know that isn't what I intended."

"I know exactly what you intended."

Between what was meant and what is, the sharks circle, ready to strike, hungry for the careless.

Or perhaps, it is just the opposite—intentions are all there is, all that matters. Intentions give hope to the postulate's faith, perspective to the artist's canvas, and defense to the lover's indiscretions. Like a pack of old cards, intent shuffles next to intent. The King and Queen know their place, the Ace struts while fearing the Trump, and the Jack of Hearts meets the forgotten Joker. I am always in search of a pair. And in such a game, I am made and stacked in piles of should.

Fictive data:

"You know I meant well."

"That's what matters most to me."

I hold my cards, deciding what to play.

Or is it that intentions wrestle their way into sense, pushing aside what seems to resist or reverse? Muscling in, they claim their space. They insist upon their own definition, their own desire, their own defense.

Fictive data:

"How do you think what you just said can be understood?"

"What I said was not intended that way. Don't put words in my mouth."

The arm bends behind, the knee pushes in, and then, the shoulders are pressed down. This is the way to a three-count, the way to twist the meaning of it all into a claim of victory. The referee refuses to raise any-one's hand.

No, intentions have no meaning from their point of origin; they only make sense from their point of destination. They are a matter of choices, options awaiting consideration.

Fictive data:

"You know that's not what I mean."

"True, but I prefer my own interpretation."

They are a matter of blindness, options that cannot be seen.

Fictive data:

"Do you see what I'm trying to say?"

"I guess I don't."

They are a matter of concern, calling forward correctives, eager for a turn.

> Fictive data:
>> "I said what I meant."
>> "Surely not."

My intentions may come to rest, then, in response. Their rivers split into two, hide beyond the bend, flood.

Awash in possibilities, I am content to find my way through the tributaries, through the flow of perhaps.

Roles and Functions

I have roles to play and functions to fulfill. Verbs need their nouns; nouns need their verbs. In the grammar of life and reason, I find my place. Phrases link to phrases, sentences rub against sentences, and conjunctions connect this with that. In the syntax of it all, the firefighter needs fire, the mail carrier needs mail, the painter needs paint. I need you and in this moment, in the middle of this unfinished sentence, you need me. The familiar script of joining together might find different form, but the coming together occurs out of habit, like having a drink, smoking a cigarette, or dropping a pill. Addicted to the known, what I can see makes me blind. Articles need their points of reference.

So, I chew on the words I put in my mouth, notice the texture, taste the seasoning. This is what I usually eat, like it or not, since this is what I have to offer. I do not ask for more. I eat with these utensils. If I leave hungry or if I starve, it is my fault, my lack of effort. I have been given more than sufficient opportunity and nourishment. This is what is being served.

> Fictive data:
>> "I want to learn what you know."
>> "Well, listen up."

I eat, unless, of course, the food for me is poison.

> Fictive data:
>> "I don't know why you have to be so resistant."
>> "I don't have a choice."

That's how I arrive, already made, accepting or fighting the flavor of it all.

I am the child whose fingers, under watchful eyes, march across the piano keyboard and the one whose stiff new shoes click against the metal chair throughout the recital. I am the parent who lives for the children I have and the one who lives forgetting the children I never knew. I am an elder rocking on the front porch who welcomes company and the one sitting still who, shocked by the memory of it all, refuses to speak.

Speech

As my feelings fall into words, as my desire finds its form, speech comes, forging forward through my vocal folds, following my breath until it finally flaunts itself in its flourish of sound. It is always an act of bravado, a boast, even in its most modest moments. Penetrating the world, it asserts a presence, a time and place. For speech is, more than anything else, an "I" tilting toward another.

Speech, that small puncture in the world's side, knows the rules and knows how to break them. Feeling bold, I might say that I am interested in its own "speechification." I am always in search of at least one knowing ear. Sometimes, I seek enough knowing ears to make a community, enough knowing ears so that I might settle safely along side nodding heads, enough so that the word is spread. Sometimes, I jabberwock along until someone gets it, until someone else claims it, until training is done. Sometimes, it just remains there like stale bread.

Fictive data:

"It sure is raining."

"Yes, the rain is rushing onto the earth's blistered rose."

Fictive data:

"It sure is raining."

"Yeah, it's raining cats and dogs."

Speech collects in people's pockets like loose coins; it is capital to be spent. I may or may not spend it well. Speech has its price.

I succumb to it and then resist. That is my only choice. That is the only way to name myself. I think of it as moving branches out of my way in the forest so that I might see. This forest is the only place where I can survive. I feel the decaying leaves under my feet.

Speakers and Listeners

More than by my intentions, my roles and functions, and my utterances, I am intertwined, for better or worse. I live in the space created by the prefix "inter": inter-weave, inter-mingle, inter-course, inter-act, inter-personal. I live in the between.

Fictive data:

"Talk to me."

"Okay."

"Let's talk about us."

"Now?"

"Yes."

"Okay."

I live there before I am interred.

Connected, I am the other's definition. Like leaf to branch, I attach by instinct and by necessity. I know of the other's spring and fall, of the other's summer and winter. I share the contents and discontents of the seasons. I communicate, breathing in what I need to survive and, at the same time, breathing in the toxic.

I cannot not communicate, unless, of course, there is no listener to give a damn, and unless, of course, the listener's punctuation has reached its final period. By speaking, I put into motion a demand. By listening, the listener accepts.

Fictive data:

"Do you know what?"

"What?"

It's a ticket for entry, each into the other's space. And, I am linked by the force of what we state, question, and promise. We perform each other into existence, acting upon and accomplishing our aims. Our acts matter, at least for that moment in time when we come together, negotiating, as we do, that space between us, fighting, as we sometimes do, over those places where our heads collide and our fists form, and joining together, as we sometimes do, in bodily embrace.

Fictive data:

"I hate you."

"I hate you, too."

Fictive data:

"I love you."

"I love you, too."

And in such claims, communication finds its genesis. In such claims, I locate my motives in the drama and comedy of it all. In such claims, I stumble upon my grammar.

Gender, Sexuality, Class, Race, Etc.

Marked, I am nothing more than a demographic label. Privileged, I am nothing more than a type. Trapped, I am nothing beyond.

Fictive data:

"That's what I would expect from someone like you."

"That is and is not a satisfactory explanation."

I am and am not a man who works against deploying his power. I am a man doing the best I know how. I keep that claim as my excuse.

Disclosure

Fictive data:

"Tell me what you are thinking."

"I'm thinking that I shouldn't tell you what I'm thinking."

The hibiscus opens to its full beauty only after days of deciding whether it's ready. In my slow unfolding, I wait before my stories leak out. And as I tell tales that tell me, I listen so that I might hear myself, and I watch how my stories are taken in. Some are met with concerned or understanding nods, some with cautious or questioning hands, and some with dismissing and angry eyes. When all of my stories are told, I have nothing left but the hope of charity.

Disclosure hands power to the listener. One might use what is being said, not to help the poor hapless fool who decided to share, but for one's own advantage. Disclosure is available as a mouse is to a cat—it's a thing to toy with until bored and a thing to bring to those one might want to please. Used for amusement and advantage, one can wait. Or, it serves as food for the starving gazelle that is frightened and separated from its kind. It protects the gazelle's slender neck and praises its annulated horns. Or, it comes as a burden. It's a heavy load on the back of an old mule that must negotiate a rocky mountain path. One false step and all will be lost.

Fictive data:

"Well, that's what I'm feeling. What do you think?"

"Quite honestly, I was hoping that you'd say what you did."

Feedback

It is food for food, feeding back after it's been fed. It is an exchange between the hungry. It is butter to bread, a relationship, once formed, inseparable. For whatever is said finds its nourishment in response. It may arrive as an appetizer, signaling the promise of more to come. It may show up as a soup, hot and hearty or tepid and thin. It may be the meat and potatoes, what everything is built around. It may draw near as a dessert, sweet and lingering or even tart. Sometimes it comes on a large platter, leaving room for more, and sometimes it arrives on a small saucer, leaving room for little else. But most important, it is prepared by different chefs, some that seem to matter and some that don't. It is always mine to swallow.

Fictive data:

"Please don't say what I think you are going to say."

"I have to."

Corrective feedback comes like a knife. It's easier to be spoon-fed. Beware of what is forked over. Everyone has another turn.

Tacit Assumptions

It is a rock half buried in the sand, worn smooth from the repetition of waves. It is something to move around, something to rub up against, and something to forget and to remember.

Fictive data:

> "Frank's coming."
>
> "I figured."
>
> "Three days."
>
> "Longer than usual."
>
> "Yes."

In the knowing, I settle into the shifting sands. Everything and nothing stays the same. The ox pulls the plow. The rain falls. I continue to live. And when all is said and done, I will be shocked by how I carried on.

Hidden, assumptions are too present. Frozen, assumptions move around. Buried, assumptions live on. Exposure is a just a matter of when the questions might emerge. Who is the taker of the granted?

Fictive data:

> "Oh, hi. How are you?"
>
> "Fine, thanks. How about you?"
>
> "Fine."
>
> "Good."
>
> "Good to see you."
>
> "Good to see you, too."

Who grants what can be taken? Who takes the taken?

Rhetoric

Whatever it is, it isn't mere. For even in its most mundane, its most bombastic, its most hollow, it matters. Between Plato's ideal and the idea, between Aristotle's sorting and the name, rhetoric races along, maneuvering this way and that, until it positions the people it needs to place.

Fictive data:

> "Well, if you believe that, then you have to believe what I've said."
>
> "I guess you've got me there."

It is the getting there, getting words to do journey's work. And upon arrival, the tourist that I am sees me seeing what I've already seen or seeing what I've never seen before. I leave home so that I might return again, pleased with where I reside. Or, I venture out so that I might find a new place to live, a place that accommodates how I have grown. I am always looking to live in a safe house.

Fictive data:

"That makes sense to me."

"I'm glad, since I'm happy with it as well."

"Good. Let's celebrate."

When applause comes, I know my safe house has been built, complete with thick insulation and brick walls, ready to withstand whatever huffing and puffing that might come its way.

Rhetoric is, after all, an art that creates worlds for contemplation and action. Rhetoric is, when it is working best, a strategic poem pulled from the heart.

Fictive data:

"The fifteen year old, raped by her father, who ponders whether or not to bring her unwanted child into her violent world, survives in her dark secret like a black rose struggling to bloom."

Situated

My talk is a just a drop in the cultural and linguistic bucket. It always depends on more than is there. It sits *in situ*, a circumstance from which it cannot separate. Its situation completes its form and function, like a period at the end of a sentence or like a car on a highway. Its context tells its who, as in "Put on your white robe," said to a young boy in the children's church choir, to a grand marshal of a graduation ceremony, or to a member of the Klan. Its context tells its why, as in "If you go out that door, don't come back," said the teacher to the student, said the parent to the child, or said the wife to the husband. Its context tells its what, as in "I love you," said by the newly wedded, by the couple celebrating their fiftieth anniversary, by the divorcees leaving the courthouse.

Situated in the familiar, I usually know just where everything goes. There, I am like a person who can knit a shawl almost without looking.

There, fingers move precisely, working needles so that they converge at just the right points. Situated in the unfamiliar, I struggle to get it right, to see what needs to be done, to take control. There, I am, like a neophyte with needles, clumsy, messy, and even dangerous. Situated in between, I search for patterns already made. I don't want to let a stitch slip.

Nested, my speech is ready to give birth.

> Fictive data:
>
> "I want to say something to you."
>
> "Okay. What?"
>
> "I think you know."
>
> "Yes. I think I do. About Dad?"
>
> "Yes."
>
> "I know what you want to say."
>
> "Okay."

Out of context, a still birth, a child's first attempts with a fork, a mis-take.

Style

It may come in a flourish, striking and full of flowers, a sundry of surprises and fanciful fragrances, scandalously sauntering about until it seems little more might be said, but it forges further, flaring into its own frivolity and satiating its own savage appetite, which few, except perhaps only others predisposed to such shamefulness, find satisfactory. Such excesses always demand notice. Or, it may be short and simple. To the point, it insists. Or, it may be pedestrian, doing its duty, getting the job done, serviceable as a shovel or a nail. Or, it may unfold like a poem, slowly revealing itself until it wraps its naked body around another's.

My style is a habit, a way of proceeding. It marks my identity like a face stamped on a coin. Its signature is a sign of my presence, sliding into the open. Style loops around the listener to see its fit. Some styles seem to be cut from the same cloth as my own garb and some from a rough, foreign fabric. It is a matter of comfort. Some styles are just what I need and some I can do without. It is a matter of measurement. Some styles work and some don't. It is a matter of easy or hard work.

Fictive data:

> "Please don't put it like that."

> "How would you have me put it?"

My style is a predisposition, a choice held in check by my limited skill.

Conflict

It starts as friction, the resistance to motion of two moving bodies. Tension rises as their surfaces rub against one another. Lines form as they scrape, scour, and scratch. They grind into heat. Pressure produces pressure; force precipitates force; energy takes energy. Before long, they are inflamed. Set in opposition, they will continue until they are ash.

Fictive data:

> "Why do you do that?"

> "Do what?"

> "Don't try and play innocent. You know what you are doing."

> "Oh please! Not this again."

> "Well, why don't you take responsibility for your actions?"

> "I can't deal with this. I'm going to get a drink."

As contention becomes clash, there are no winners, no protagonists. It is a contest with few rules. Don't give in. Attack where vulnerable. Use silence as your final weapon. Be petty. It really is quite easy. Play until your opposition is no longer in sight, until you have protected what you think matters, until the bitter end.

Once the game ends, I live in regret. It never feels satisfying to win.

Empathy

Once, it was in fashion to try to feel with and to understand another person. It was a friend's proof of friendship, a lover's testament to love, a therapist's guide to therapy. It was an act of giving, of generosity, of grace. It was food in the pockets of the starving.

Fictive data:

> "So, I just don't know where to turn."

"I think I know how you are feeling."

Now, it is considered presumptuous, an impossible act, given individual differences. It is to think that White might understand Black or that Black might understand White. It is to believe that one might color within the lines.

    Fictive data:

        "So, I just don't know where to turn."

        "I think I know how you are feeling."

        "No, you don't. You can't."

Or, even worse, it is a predatory act that names with the use of one's own vocabulary. It makes the other into oneself. Four and twenty blackbirds baked into a pie.

    Fictive data:

        "So, I just don't know where to turn."

        "I think I know how you are feeling."

        "No, you don't. You can't."

        "I think I do. You are just feeling . . . ."

Or, perhaps, it is a cathartic pleasure, a release from the obligation to act. A tear for a tear washes away any guilt.

    Still, I cannot deny my desire and the need to participate in another life, to share in another person's feelings of joy and sorrow. I cannot escape from empathy's call. Such a desire and need lets me be fully human, lets me find my other half.

Apprehension

Slowly, apprehension settles in—anxiety's ache, tension's throb. It nestles in to stay, to take control, to name its terms. It keeps my body from listening to the head. It insists I communicate about being afraid to communicate. It is my chemical mishap. It is my worry worrying.

    I carry fear because communication matters. I realize that what I might say has consequences. I live in anticipation of verdict. My quivering voice and shaking hands try to quiver and shake their way around cold eyes. They never succeed. They are noticed, even when some claim they were not. That voice and those hands say more than what is being said.

> Fictive data:
>> "I don't know why I was so nervous."
>>
>> "I didn't even notice."
>
> Fictive data:
>> "I don't know why he was so nervous."
>>
>> "I just wanted his misery to end."

My heart pounds because the most meaningful communication comes from the heart. Sweat pours because the most meaningful communication I sweat about. The mouth dries because the most meaningful communication takes the moisture of connection.

Self-assessment

When talking, I often listen to what comes out. At times, I might be fully entertained by my own chatter; at other times, appalled. Added together with all the times in between, I find the basis for self-assessment. It determines how I move through the world, ready or reticent, depending upon the situation, to communicate. It establishes the degree to which I see speech as a potential or a pitfall. Seen as an opportunity, the world is made of ready words; seen as a quagmire, the world is made in foreign tongues.

> Fictive data:
>> "I don't know how to say what I want to say."
>>
>> "Let me see if I can put it in words for you."

The manager of meaning manages all. The owner of words always ranks highest on one's own scale.

When talking, I often hear the squeak and squeal of it all. The voice works with and beside language. My body feels language's lightness and its weight. By attending to the how, self-assessments gain strength. Measuring good and bad is constant, ongoing. I am never without my own watchful eye, never without judgment.

Fictive data:

"I don't like how that came out."

"I can see why you wouldn't."

When talking, often I know how it all falls out.

Efficacy

Change comes from communication and communication comes from change. Both count. Or should it be said, the lack of change causes communication and communication causes the lack of change.

Fictive data:

"We never do anything anymore."

"I like how we live our lives."

Both negotiate loss. Or perhaps, the call for change is a call for communication, setting into motion, as it does, agendas for action, agendas, if they are to be achieved, that require talk.

Communication's power to produce an effect is more than an isolated growl in the woods. It makes the woods habitable. It tames the dark, buries the acorn, and makes shelter from fallen branches. It cuts paths to follow, some smooth as a shining leaf and some rough as splintered bark.

Fictive data:

"Now I see what we need to do."

"Good. I think it's important that we go that way."

Communication keeps me from being lost. It offers me a way to go.

Chapter 3
Struggling for Speech

Incident 1: We had been married for five years when it happened. Like most couples, we had our ups and downs, but I believed we had a long future in front of us, a future that included our two-year-old son who we both thought, as parents do, was just wonderful. We were renting a lovely house and enjoying our first real jobs and the money that came along with them. And although I knew we were both too young when we married, and I knew I wasn't what I'd call the ideal husband, we seemed to be moving along as couples do. The day it happened we had decided to take in a film, the Barbra Steisand and Robert Redford romance, *We Way We Were*. I was sitting there waiting for the film to start and tossing popcorn into my mouth, when I realized she was crying. "What's the matter?" I asked, confused. "I want a divorce," she answered.

Incident 2: I hate giving back graded papers. Not only do they require more work than I enjoy giving them, they seldom seem to be the learning opportunities for students that I wish they would be. I must admit I get discouraged when I see students get a paper back, flip to the last page to see the grade, and then throw the paper away without even bothering to read my comments. That isn't how it's supposed to work. Nor did it work the way I had hoped when Michael (fictive name) came into my office to discuss his graded paper. I was slowly moving through the paper trying to explain the comments I had made. There were plenty, perhaps more than I should have given. The writing was poor and the ideas, as best I could tell, were not very compelling. Michael seemed to be following me, seemed to be taking in what I was offering. He was nodding his head, listening. I thought we were working well. Then, leaning back in his chair and pointing to back of his brown hand, he said, "I know why I got the grade I got." The implication was clear.

Incident 3: When I play golf, I want to play with someone who knows the rules, who is ready to hit when his/her turn comes, and who is serious but still recognizes it is only a game. Frank (fictive name) is such a player. I've enjoyed for many years playing with him and having a few beers after the round. I love how he would laugh when he didn't hit the shot he wanted. He was a good partner. I also knew from little things said here and there that he and I didn't share much in common in the way of politics or religion, but that didn't much matter on the golf course. One day, after we both had rounds that we were feeling pretty good about, we sat in the clubhouse telling each other what we already knew: "That shot on sixteen was just short of being out of bounds." "I can't believe I missed that two-footer on twelve." "I loved that five iron I hit from the rough on number six."

After we had downed a couple of Heinekens and analyzed our round from every angle, Frank inched his chair closer to mine and looked me straight in the eyes. "I have something to ask you."

"What's that, Frank?" I said, knowing this wasn't going to be a golf question.

"Don't you want to be praising Jesus when you die?"

In this essay, I explore those disruptive moments in interpersonal interactions when a person is forced to find communicative strategies for dealing with the unexpected, when one just doesn't know how to respond. I am particularly interested in those times when both the speaker and listener feel that what is said next in the ongoing communicative exchange and, perhaps, in their relationship, is of utmost importance. Such communicative moments have been addressed by a number of scholars under a number of related labels, e.g., social predicaments (Cupach, 1994), embarrassing circumstances (Miller, 1992), conversational dilemmas (Daly, Diesel & Weber, 1994), awkward silences (McLaughlin & Cody, 1982), defensiveness (Stamp, Vangelisti & Daly, 1992), "nexting" (Stewart, 2009), and remedial interchange (Goffman, 1971). Recognizing the frequency in which people find themselves facing these tricky communicative events, some writers (e.g., Guilmartin,

2002; Chödrön, 2001) have offered self-help books to provide speakers with the language they might need in a given circumstance. Yet, neither the scholarship nor the self-help books offer an account of the phenomenological experience of the moment when one realizes that he or she is in a difficult communicative situation. Having described three such moments, I turn to a poetic phenomenology to write my experience.

In the first incident described above, I found myself trying to comfort my former wife. I saw the person I loved upset, and I wanted to help, even after she said, with tears pouring down her face, that she was leaving to be with my friend Tom. A day later, she moved out. In the second incident, after recovering from what I read as an accusation, I said, "Our conference is over now. You have to leave my office." Michael never returned to class. In the third incident, my flippant response, "I'm afraid if I were praising Jesus when I died, he would just see me as a hypocrite," was met with, "That is just why you need to change your ways." Frank, a man who I saw as only a good golfing buddy, was genuinely concerned about my immortal soul. I ended our conversation by saying, "Frank, I don't want to talk with you about this." Although we've played many rounds of golf together since then, Frank never brought the subject up again.

With each of these incidences, I am asked to perform, to provide a response suitable to the moment. As I struggle for speech, I find myself physically and psychologically *heightened*, momentarily *speechless*, feeling *inadequate* to the task, but with a *surplus* of possible actions, *torn* between my own and the other's concerns, *doubled*, and *wondering*.

Heightened

Your body quickens, sits more upright, stands more erect. Your hands are birds on an unsteady branch. Thrown into readiness, your pulse increases. Your head pulls back, turtle to shell. Adrenaline rushes. Alert, you are living in the moment, in the instant before the unavoidable wreck, in the split second the glass falling from your grasp hits the floor. Your stomach turns. You are both the cat in anticipation of the mouse and the mouse in anticipation of the cat. Ready to pounce or be pounced upon, the body, tense, taut, is triggered, available for use. Alarmed, with your keen eyed, diligent stillness, you remain on guard, knowing that at a time too soon to come, you must act.

Speechless

Your tongue refuses your heart's desire. You want safe words, healing words, right words, but nothing and everything taunts as possibilities. You swallow. Your tongue searches, probes for the one phrase that might satisfy. But nothing will do. Stunned into silence, it settles, aching for use. Your tongue wants your words, and it can't decide if it should arch up, slip along, or push against. It is lost in its dark cavern. You wonder why you cannot speak, why your tongue languishes in its damp chamber, alone, eager but useless as a sleeping snail. You want it to have a point, to be serviceable as a match to a candle.

You know that words matter. Words can save, rescue the desperate. Words can adventure, risk the dangerous. Words can comfort, please the moment. But when none are to be found, words betray. They are the butterflies escaping the net, the cup too small to hold its drink, the worm on July concrete.

Inadequate

There is an expectancy of response. Thrust on stage, you are a character struggling for lines from a drama yet to be written. There have been no rehearsals, no trial runs, no previews. You are a novice in an unknown genre. You have no script for this opening night. The curtain has parted and the lights are blinding. Center stage, you consider moving stage right or stage left. You want to exit, but know you cannot. You are being watched. No one can prompt you. No one can take your place. It is your role to perform. You have been cast against your will. You know you must act, must answer the eyes.

Eyes want you to begin, to take them out of their discomfort. They stare at you, look down, and then stare at you again. You want to meet them eye to eye, but you are stopped by what you've seen and stopped by what you are trying to see. There is no clear vision. You are hobbled, hollow, helpless. You are small, shaken, senseless. Everything is a blur. The eyes wait.

Surplus

Ideas, like prairie dogs, pop up and then run underground. None hold still, except for a quick moment. And in that moment, there is hope of connection, but they soon bury themselves again. There are just too many, too many rushing here and there, too many to contain.

Ideas, like marbles spilling from a bag, run everywhere.

Ideas, like autumn leaves, are more than you expect. And in the demanding wind, they swirl out of control.

Ideas, like a pot boiling over, make a mess. Now, there is no time for cleaning up. Everything is too hot.

And after the rush and push of all their promises, ideas, like wounded soldiers, lie still. They spill the blood of failure. Their limbs hang heavy at their sides, confused by their inability to move. Shattered, they know they are of no use. They live among their comrades (too many to count), who once thought they could make a difference. They fall into ash.

Torn

There is no answer or no answer that you can find quickly enough that seems appropriate to the moment. Someone must be sacrificed—you or them. You know that they have spoken out of need, spoken, perhaps, out of a concern for you. You see their pain, their anxiety, their worry. You want to allow yourself to go to them, to be supportive, to take away their uneasiness. But, to do so, you know you will betray yourself. Your anger, sadness, frustration, shock, and outrage cannot language their need. You do not want to be insensitive, cruel, or unreasonable. You do not want to deny what you are feeling. You matter. They matter. The choice pulls from both sides, tightening around you. It cuts into your skin. It always leaves its mark.

When trapped, the fox considers chewing off its paw. There is no escape from pain.

Doubled

You watch yourself speaking, saying things that are hard to hear. You are both yourself and outside yourself. You have been kicked out of the sanctuary of your own body, but there you are, struggling to make sense of it all. You are glad that you are not the hapless and inept you you see before you. You want to help yourself, but you remain removed, a distant, cold parent who eyes disapprovingly. You see yourself grappling for something to hold on to, but you do not extend a hand. You observe and wait for the outcome. And then, you see yourself floating above it all, looking down. You wonder why you do not offer yourself any assistance, any kind words of advice. You are frustrated that you are of such little use, yet this curious other you appears to have escaped the moment, and hovers safely, out of harm's way. You would like to join yourself, drift away, but you cannot. You are here and you are there. You cannot come together. Later, you may be able to pick up the pieces.

Wondering

After everything is said and done, it is not done. Answers frighten and questions haunt. Its ghostly presence drags through the night. Perhaps, there might have been another way—rat's tail or mole's hair—a way that would calm the spirits. Perhaps, you could conjure up the scene again, summon a different brew. Perhaps, your ghastly self could rematerialize, fresh and innocent. But second chances are a dark hope. The warts are yours to keep.

The Empty Essence

The mind spins and the body tenses. Speech goes. Then, it comes in an avalanche of waste, offers too many options, none of which satisfy. All involved are left questioning. Such interpersonal moments disrupt, call upon the impromptu, and place into suspicion communicative competence.

The symptoms are clear, but there is no cure, no three steps from a 101 textbook. Words will come, an exchange will occur, and actions will be taken, but no planning, no careful execution, and no meaningful gestures will please the moment. At best, whatever is said and done is our best. Situations that carry consequences are often ripe with possibilities. I live the best I can knowing that choosing matters.

Chapter 4
Relational Associations

I write by association—one thought triggering the next to illustrate how interpersonal schemes come into play, to show the interconnectedness of sense-making, to tell how the accumulation of experiences creates a sense of self. I write by remembering, sometimes accurately and sometimes with skewed vision, but always recording what I believe to be true. I write for logics that will hold steady, for stories I want to carry, for claims I can use.

The simple greeting:

> "Hi, how are you?"

> "Fine. How about yourself?

> "Fine."

finds its meaning in its bodily performance (e.g., the meeting or diverting of eyes, the smiling or blank face, the opening or closing of arms, the lasting or perfunctory hug) and in its vocal articulation (e.g., the warmth of deep tones or the cautionary clipped sounds that signal watching, the pace that says I do want to know how you are or the one that says I must be moving on, the playful tease that mocks the ritual or the formality of social pleasantry). When we exchanged those words signaling that we were here despite all the sad history we carried, I knew we were here to stay.

Place takes its shape with its inhabitants. In my childhood homes on Milan and Agate Streets in New Orleans, I see my parents. There's my mom on Milan Street. She is tending Jackson the parakeet in the small kitchen and there she is again crying the first tears I ever saw her shed the day he died. There's my dad coming up the steep stairs after a long day at work and me rushing to greet him: "What did you bring me?" I'm there sitting in the small foyer playing with the trinket he brought. There I am with Mom on Agate Street positioned at the kitchen table, cutting carrots for dinner, while she moves about readying the meal for Dad's arrival. And there is Dad, tossing rubber circles at a hook board, accumulating more points than anyone who might dare to challenge him. I hear him offering me good counsel: "Never bet a man playing his own game in his own home." And many years later I see them in their condo at Mariners' Cove after all the children were gone, and after Katrina struck, displaced in a small apartment in Lake Charles.

In each place I've lived people appear. There's Bill, my first roommate, sharing with me our small dorm room, and there's Bill again, as wide-eyed as I am, listening outside our off-campus apartment to a woman who lives just two doors away explain that she doesn't work, that she has an arrangement with a man who takes care of her needs. There is my first wife in our small apartment in Dallas and in the large log cabin in Blacksburg, the one we occupied before she left, needing a new home where she felt it would be easier for her to give her love. There is my drill sergeant, checking up and down the rows of the barracks to see if our beds were sufficiently made while we all stood at nervous attention, and there is Chuck, my best friend from Vietnam, dealing cards in our hooch. There is the apartment of my graduate school days where too many came in and out and my apartment in Detroit, a part of a mega-complex that had its own grocery store and hair salon, where I nodded to neighbors but knew no one.

My wife is there in my homes of the last thirty years, from our first rented house on top of a small hill where we were married, to the house in the woods where a copperhead snake crawled around the same floor that our young daughter did, to our two houses, one on Wedgewood and then the next on Frances, that proved we earned a good wage. In these houses are years of history, years of making a life together.

Presence turns space into place. It says here people reside, come together and, sometimes, come apart.

Seldom is there sadness when people come together, connect; often sadness shapes coming apart, even in cases when all involved know it is for the best. Coming apart seems like a failure, a lost opportunity. Potential is unfulfilled or exhausted. Blame may be shared or directed at oneself or the other. The more the pointing finger is put into play, the less the curling finger says come here.

"Come sit by me," I said.

"I'd rather not," she replied.

"Why not?"

"Because I'm not liking you very much right now," she noted.

"But if you stay over there, we can't hold hands, and if we can't hold hands, you'll always be over there," I said.

"Maybe over here is where I want to be," she answered.

"That would be a sad choice," I said, waiting to see what she would do.

"I've spent my life waiting for your mother," I said to my daughter. "Have you noticed how when we've decided to leave someplace, your mother will take forever saying goodbye? Or whenever we are ready to go someplace, your mother has to get a drink or put on lipstick? Have you noticed?" My daughter laughed, recognizing the pattern. "On my gravestone will be the words: 'His life was spent waiting for the woman he loved.'"

My wife, listening to our conversation, laughed, too. "Would you prefer I rush?"

"Oh no," I answered, "it is always my pleasure to see just how long it might take you." But behind the teasing, behind the laughter, she recognized some truth, and she became more mindful whenever I was waiting.

Being mindful is an act of listening, of watching. It requires alert attention. It demands presence. It operates by understanding the fragility of connection. It knows what is at stake, what matters.

"Do I matter to you?" she asked.

"Of course, you matter to me," was my quick reply.

"Look at me. Look at me and tell me that I matter."

I turned towards her: "You matter to me."

"Sometimes I think I'm pretty low on your list—I feel like I come behind your work, sports on TV, your mother, and God knows what else."

I pointed the remote at the television and turned it off. I knew it was time for talk. The game, score tied, was in the last quarter.

Games bring us together. We share watching, playing, commenting—it's usually safe, usually engaging, usually an escape, usually a release.

"You shithead! I can't believe you went out with gin," she said, even though she was forty-seven points ahead.

"Did I get you with lots of big ones?" I answered, hoping I was back in the game.

"I don't think I can count this high," she remarked, putting down her cards. Whether we are playing gin, pool, or golf or watching one of our favorite teams, we have one implicit and fruitful rule: No talking about the office. For us, games mark relational time, establish an "our."

Sometimes games become battlefields for other issues: "You shithead!" Then, games keep us apart. We fall into patterns, set up tests of affection, hint at but never say what is of concern.

"Would you cover my foot with the blanket?" I asked her.

She was sitting on the other end of the sofa and considered my request. "This foot?" she said, lifting the cover.

"Yes, that one."

She dropped the blanket so that both of my feet were exposed. "How's that?"

"Not what I was I was hoping for."

"Do you think I'm your servant who will answer to your every desire?"

"No, but I was hoping you'd cover my foot," I said, watching her.

"You can't cover it yourself?"

"Yes, I can. I didn't think I was asking much."

"Well, maybe, it was more than I wanted to do."

"I guess it was." I pull my legs back from her side of the couch and place my feet on the floor. "I'm going to get bowl of ice cream. Do you want something?"

"No, not now," she says, but we both know there is never an escape from desire.

Desire: that initial attraction, that assessment that says yes, possibly you, possibly us; that emergent passion that loops around anticipation in the heady excitement of perhaps now; that happy hope of an us, yes, again us; that steady settling, committed to a future, to a taken-for-granted, of course, coupled we; that history that claims the impossibility of separation, even if separation might come, a history that insists on together.

Together, we sip memories like soup, hot in the mouth, thickened from the accumulation of days. We stir as if remembering is our appetizer for love. Our lives are seasoned. Our past sizzles with heat. We serve the promise of tomorrow.

The promise of "I do," publicly offered and available only to some, is a statement of worth. It is, as Fred Flintstone might say, a yabba dabba (I) doo moment, or, to put a more cynical spin on it, an occasion when one says to another you are good enough. We take each others' measurements and decide—yes, you; no, not you. And in the exchange, we come to see the cost and the reward, calculated by counterbalancing ourself and the other on a variable scale. In such a system, who falls short? Who seems lacking? Who just picks him/herself? Marriage, that selfish pleasure, is the promise of "I gain."

We find our pleasure most often in what we call our "perfect normal." In the perfect normal, our hands join as we walk into a restaurant; we rest one hand on the other's leg while sitting on the sofa; we give a short massage as we stand in line. In the perfect normal, talk is easy, without worry, enriched by years of sharing. Words are taken in, enjoyed, held with appreciation and care. Conversation flows with the confidence of tomorrow. In the perfect normal, pleasure comes from the labor of seeing.

The first time I saw her she stood at the top of the stairs. She was joking with several of her friends, and I was just walking by. But I noticed: she held attention as she turned this way and that to bring everyone in. She was thin, almost boyish, but with a deep, almost hidden, sensual femininity. Her smile told of her wit, her sly quickness. She was taking in how others were processing her remarks. I do not know if she noticed that I went by—I would like to think so. I knew then that I was more than interested. I made inquiries. She was not currently with anyone. I placed myself in a position where we might interact. We danced. I was hers. She acted indifferent, but she noticed.

Indifference comes without desire; indifference comes concealing desire.

Indifference is a cold weapon, a cutting blow below the belt, used as a statement against history.

Indifference is a failure to stop, to look, sometimes driven by efficiency or practicality and sometimes indicative of status or ego. Its result is to erase.

Indifference arises out of comfort, the taken-for-granted. It notices the difference when the familiar fades.

Indifference, finding everything equal, speaks in a monotone, moves at the same pace. Its signature is print.

Indifference doesn't care.

"How could you do that if you cared about me?"

"I care about you."

"Your actions sure don't make me think so."

"What did you expect me to do?"

"I expected you to think of me."

"I wasn't thinking."

"Obviously not."

"I'm sorry."

"I'm not sure if sorry is enough. I'm not sure if I'll ever be able to forgive you or if I want to forgive you. How could you do that to us?"

When a colleague wrote to the dean, the vice president of academic affairs, and the president of the university that I was unethical because I voted on the tenure case of one faculty in the same year that my wife was up for tenure, I could not forgive him. He had first brought the issue up to the faculty and everyone argued that his concerns were not valid— we were not under any quota system; we were not comparing which of the two candidates had greater merit; I would not be present during the discussion of my wife's file. The faculty decided I had the right and obligation to vote, and so I did. Despite their decision, he felt he was right and took it upon himself to express his perspective beyond the walls of the department. When the letter he sent found its way into my hands, I felt wounded and wronged. My departmental chair, after we discussed what should be done, sent a corrective letter to all concerned. Formally, the problem went no further, but I spent much of my career holding a grudge. He became someone who I marked as an enemy. Initially, we did not speak to each other. As the years passed, we might exchange perfunctory greetings but nothing more. He retired and left the department. Our relationship was never repaired.

I may be wrong but I do not believe I have more than a usual number of enemies. All that I do have, I regret. I find myself considering what I might have done differently. I enact scripts in my head that might remove an individual from my enemies list. I trust that talk might turn hostility into, if not friendship, quiet. But with some, I have not given talk a chance to work. I know I should. I know the energy it takes to stay angry, to keep someone in negative space. I know I have wronged others and wanted forgiveness. Sometimes I was forgiven, sometimes not. I know that forgiveness is an act of generosity. I know that we all have our own self-serving narratives.

I story my life to make it hold still, to hold on. My stories place me with others under the spotlight, exposed. An acquaintance, after reading some of my work, asked: "How can you write all that stuff about yourself?" I took her question to mean how could I disclose the intimate details of my life. My first reaction was one of surprise: I did not realize that I was being overly disclosive. I shared what I would have with anyone who might be interested. Then, I thought: I share what it means for me to be human in the hope that by writing my life, others might find a place of resonance or resistance.

Perhaps, however, her question was an ethical one: how could you implicate others as you wrote about yourself? In my defense I would simply say: I am nothing more than my interactions with others. To write is to name others, to bring history forward. To listen, as I write, is my ethical burden. My task is to remember what Russell (2009) learned on pilgrimage: "compassion is the only healing power we truly possess" (p. 601). Perhaps, then, I might write with sensitivity, with an invitational ear.

I realized I felt him in my life as a burden. It seemed he was always in need, always asking for something, always making demands. I could not shake the feeling—he was a weight, a stone I was ready to drop. You are a selfish ass, I told myself. I can't walk away. I can't turn my back on him. He is my friend. I would continue doing what I had been doing and I would continue feeling him as a burden. He would know, but we would never mention it.

"We will always have that elephant in the room," she said. "I won't mention it again, but it will always be there."

"Perhaps the elephant might go in the closet," I answered. "Or better yet, in the yard. Maybe a neighbor would keep it."

"This isn't something to joke about."

"My point is that I don't want to live with it. I look forward to the time when that damn elephant dies and we can bury it together."

"Mom is dying," Jan blurted out. "We have to accept that."

"She isn't going to die," Lilly, her sister, shot back. "Not now, anyway. The doctors said she has a fighting chance, and we all know she is a fighter."

"They were just trying to ease us into acceptance. They're not going to take away all hope."

"Why are you always so pessimistic?"

"I'm not being pessimistic; I'm being realistic."

"I'll choose another reality."

"It's not always that easy. What we need to be thinking about is where we want to bury her."

"Stop," Lilly insisted. "You have to stop now."

Jan turned away, but she was thinking about who she needed to call. I followed her out the room, knowing my job was simply to be there.

"You okay?" I asked.

"Yes. I just don't know why everyone is deluding themselves when we have things to do. We need to call my brother."

"Call him. Let him know what's going on, but then, let's just see how everything unfolds. We'll have plenty of time for making check marks."

"Should I call some funeral homes?"

"Not now. No need to do that now."

"I don't want Mom to die," she said, bursting into tears.

"I know," I replied, taking her into my arms.

My tears might come when I'm watching a film, a stage performance, or even a television commercial. Often such tears seem less about the object of my attention and more about some emotional build-up from some other aspects of my life. These tears might best be described as a poignant bowel movement. They serve as a needed release.

My tears also flow when human suffering, in all its various forms, is present, particularly if the pain is connected to someone I love. But the tears I shed that surprised me, that still haunt me, that keep me living in doubt are the tears that ran down my face when I turned my back on my son.

"Hey, Dad. It's me. Doug," he began.

I could tell something was wrong by the tone of his voice, but I could have easily guessed since he only called when he found himself in trouble. "Hey, Doug. What's up?"

"I'm in jail, Dad. I got picked up for driving while suspended," he reported. "You've got to get me out."

"Driving while suspended? I thought you got that problem

straightened out. That's what I gave you that money for last spring." My head was racing with thoughts: in the last six months, I had given him money for the lawyer, money when he needed a new car, and money when he found himself homeless. Tough love, everyone repeatedly advised. He's thirty-eight years old, and he needs to be responsible for himself.

"The lawyer said everything was taken care of but I guess he didn't do it."

"Doug, that's hard for me to believe." Seldom did I find myself believing him. His stories always seemed a bit off, a bit of a con, but often with enough truth that I felt compelled to help. That's what good cons do—they make you believe them, friends and family told me.

"That's what he said," Doug insisted.

"Then you need to get your money back."

"I can't if I'm in jail, and I need $3,000 to get out."

"$3,000?"

"Yeah, that's what I need to make bail."

"Doug, I feel so angry right now I don't know what to say. Every time you call, it is with some new crisis."

"I know, Dad. But this time I really need your help."

"That's what you always say, Doug."

"I'll pay you back, Dad."

"That's the other thing you always say but you never have, not once, ever." The years of broken promises and disappointments, of just-help-me-this-time, of feeling deceived, a dupe, came rushing in on me. "Look, Doug, I'm not going to help you out this time. You got yourself in this mess, you get yourself out."

"You've got to help me out, Dad. I can't stay here," he pleaded.

"I'm sorry, Doug."

"Dad, I've got to get out of here. There was this guy in the shower who already punched me in the face, just for being there. You don't know what it's like in here." He began to cry. He sounded frightened.

"I'm sorry, Doug."

"You can't leave me here, Dad."

"I'm sorry," I repeated and hung up. I was shaking.

"What's up with Doug?" Mimi, my wife, asked.

"Same old shit. He's in jail. I told him I wouldn't bail him out." And then, my sobs began—hard, violent, uncontrollable.

"You did the right thing," Mimi said, being supportive. She began rubbing my back.

"It's just so hard to turn your back on your son," I cried.

"I hate how he puts you in that position," she said.

"He's in jail," I moaned. "I told him 'no.'"

Saying no has never been easy for me. I prefer when people pick up my clues, see my hesitancy. If they don't, more often than not I'll go along rather than deploy that simple two letter word. The difference between being accommodating and being spineless is the difference between yes and yes.

Difference, marked by labels, keeps us cautious:

"I don't see how we can work. We just have too many differences."

"It will keep things interesting."

"It will keep us fighting."

Similarity, marked by labels, keeps us bored:

"You've been that way for years."

"That's right."

"As you know, I'm that way too."

"Yes, I know."

Differences and similarities, marked by labels, keep us separate in the unfounded belief that we know.

"How well do you think you know me?"

"I know you well enough to know that if I answer pretty well, you'll do something that I wouldn't expect."

"I don't ever want to be predictable."

"Only your unpredictability is predictable."

"I might change that."

"You might."

"You don't know me very well, do you?"

"I know you well enough to know that this conversation is not heading in a good direction."

"You are so smug. You think you've got me all figured out, but you don't."

"I thought I was doing pretty well."

"You asshole! Are you just trying to pick a fight?"

"Me? It's you who started all this."

"I simply asked you if you thought you knew me, and then you get all high-and-mighty."

"I was just trying to answer your questions."

"You don't know me at all."

"I give up. Just stop. I don't want to talk about this anymore."

Stop. Count to three. Be careful. Remember how Rogers (1961) encourages us to live with an attitude of acceptance, with "unconditional positive regard." Consider the situation, the circumstances. You don't want to regret what you are going to say. Your words will have consequences. You don't want to say anything that is hurtful, that will come back and bite you. Remember who is sitting there. It's someone you care about, someone you don't want to upset. Remember, too, that you have a right to say what you think. You are entitled to your feelings. You have a perspective on all this. Now, say something.

This piece is nothing but words piled next to words, sense-making constructions built on experience, always vulnerable to alternative evidence. I have nothing more and nothing less than renderings, assertions and speculations that inform my life. I am my languaging. I use what I can speak.

Chapter 5
Stephen Dunn and the Poetics of Living

I wish to start with a bold assertion: Stephen Dunn is a scholar of personal relations. I do not believe he would make such an assertion himself; more likely, he would see himself as a poet. He has written fifteen poetry books as well as two collections of essays on poetic craft. He won a Pulitzer Prize for his collection *Different Hours* and received several other prestigious poetry awards. Yet, Dunn, perhaps more than anyone else, teaches me about interpersonal relationships. I offer this analysis to show how his poetry is an inquiry, how it speaks my life, how it helps me make sense of myself and my relationships. I read his lines and find resonance, discover myself. I make this case as an example of the power of poetic expression and of the instructional work poetry can accomplish.

Dunn's poetry locates for me a constant human puzzle: How might I connect with another person when my efforts to do so seem tentative, slippery, askew, or empty? How might I satisfy my desire to fully embrace another when I confront troubling and persistent barriers? On the simplest level, Dunn suggests language hides and fails me. Hidden from others, I find myself, walking the street, remembering Dunn's descriptive lines: "Always a gesture away from contact, / Ungiven gifts, first words / It would seem foolish to say" ("This Late in the Century," *New and Selected Poems*, p. 84). This inability to speak, to reach out, this reluctance or fear to connect, writes itself again and again in my encounters with those I do not know. But even with those I share some history, hiding is prevalent. Dunn pointedly notes, "When he spoke he was charming, / Allowed everyone to enjoy / Not knowing him" ("Legacy," *New and Selected Poems*, p. 146). I have felt the power of charm, been pulled to and enjoyed its presence, and found myself wanting to reach beyond that surface glitter only to be told to stop. I, too, have used charm's seductive muscle to keep others away and relished in the slippery escape.

More disturbing, I have found myself hiding from those with whom I have been most close. Dunn reminds me of the times I have named my inadequacies as if they are gestures of intimacy when, in fact, they were nothing more than manipulative maneuvers: "You must worry about trusting a man / Who feels he's damned / And knows there's a certain charm in admitting it" ("The Overt," *Different Hours*, p. 76). Dunn tells me how such disclosures come at an interpersonal price: "For years I've known that to confess / is to say what one doesn't feel" ("Burying the Cat," *Different Hours*, p. 111), even though, "your secrets differentiate you / from no one" ("The Soul's Agents," *Everything Else in the World*, p. 36). And Dunn catches me in my most intimate moments: "Our solitudes are so populated / That sometimes after sex / We know it's best to be quiet" ("Sleeping with Others," *The Insistence of Beauty*, p. 84). After the years, after the forgettable and unforgettable moments, to touch is to be in touch with many, real and imagined, rejoicing and regretting.

Language not only lets me hide the person I would like to be, but it also fails in its representational desire. Dunn writes, "Nothing is quite what it was / after we've formed a clear picture of it" ("Burying the Cat," *Different Hours*, p. 111). Language, Dunn suggests, distorts, takes away, misrepresents, even lies:

> *...oh even*
> *the open-minded yearn for a fiction*
> *to rein things in—*
> *the snapshot, the lie of the frame.*
> ("The Reserve Side," *Different Hours*, p. 73)

Dunn recommends: "Try to practice unsettling / what remains settled in you" (The Soul's Agent," *Everything Else in the World*, p. 36). Nevertheless, I continue to try to "rein things in," to make language hold steady, and, like Dunn, to "keep on describing things / to ensure that they really happened" ("Sixty," *Different Hours*, p. 22). When I have said what I must, like Dunn, I conclude: "I used to believe in words, how they could / come together happily, and change. / Now I just pray they don't

distort" ("Letter About Myself to You," *New and Selected Poems*, p. 110).
And I, like Dunn, wonder:

> *How do we not go crazy,*
> *we who have found ourselves compelled*
> *to live with the circle, the ellipsis, the word*
> *not yet written.*
>
> ("The Reserve Side," *Different Hours*, p. 73)

My language and the tricks I make it play as well its own recalcitrance are not my only missteps. At times, I am not fully present to others, open, loving, ready or capable of genuine exchange. Dunn brings to mind those moments of pulling away when he writes:

> *Everything was clear, and nothing much*
> *the better for it.*
> *They agreed it was a matter of caring,*
>
> *and each felt the dull courage that comes*
> *from caring less.*
>
> ("Diminuendo," *Loosestripe*, p. 19)

It is always "a matter of caring," of refusing the easy escape that keeps me open to the possibility of another. When I retreat, when I seek the safety of my solitude, when I care less, I may take some comfort in the flight from obligation. I may even feel, as Dunn suggests, a "dull courage," but I never break loose from the loss. It lives in me like a swallowed stone.

Even with those I continue to share relationships, relationships I would count as my best, Dunn tells me of the emptiness that accompanies them when he offers his own postmortem guide:

> *You who are one of them, say that I loved*
> *my companions most of all.*
> *In all sincerity, say that they provided*
> *a better way to be alone.*
>
> ("A Postmortum Guide," *Different Hours*, p. 121)

In these lines, Dunn marks those moments when I have sat with friends and lovers, genuinely pleased by their presence, even needing their presence and, at the same time, aware of myself as disconnected, wanting more, wanting to get beyond the disheartening drag of the everyday, wanting the words that might penetrate. Dunn laments: "Oh, if we didn't know who we are / and what we've become / We could believe in a paradise" ("This Far Out in the Country," *Loosestripe*, p. 28). Too often, I find myself stopping on the edge of promise.

Dunn helps me remember the difficulty of life, of how its pleasures never come without entanglements, dark surprises, and disruptions. At best, I say, borrowing from Dunn, to those I love, "I will try to disappoint you / Better than anyone ever has" ("Mom Semblable," *New and Selected Poems*, p. 230). I know that despite my best efforts, I will disappoint, will prove again and again that my best efforts are always inadequate. Such awareness saddens, but, nevertheless, keeps me wanting to be there, facing another, trying. And in the trying, I have "learned to live / with pleasure's ache" and "intimacy's concealments" ("Goethe in Galloway Township," *Local Visitations*, p. 84). At worst, I simply disappoint. Dunn writes:

> *It's in disappointment we look for words*
> *to convince us*
> *the spaces between stars are nothing*
> *to worry about*
> . . .
> *And the words we find*
> *are always insufficient, like love*
> *though they are often lovely*
> *and all we have.*
>
> ("Those of Us Who Think We Know,"
> *New and Selected Poems*, p. 58)

In Dunn's construction, I am the disillusioned fool, dressed in deceit, unable to speak into the dark, believing too much in words. "How unlucky we humans are," Dunn notes, "doomed to know what we've done" ("Explanations," *Everything Else in the World*, p. 88). But, I am also the one trying, struggling to celebrate the joy that words allow. And so, with Dunn, I believe:

> *Because finally the personal*
> *is all that matters,*
> *we spend years describing stones,*
> *chairs, abandoned farmhouses—*
> *until we're ready. Always*

> *it's a matter of precision,*
> *what it feels like*
> *to kiss someone or to walk*
> *out the door. How good it was*
> *to practice on stones*
> *which were things we could love*
> *without weeping over.*
>
> ("Essay on the Personal," *New and Selected Poems*, p. 139)

Dunn teaches me that it is in the weeping promise resides. Although relationships carry their difficulties, "the personal is all that matters."

> *And so we live now*
> *with the door open, the heart*
> *learning about the fullness and ache*
>
> *that comes from letting in.*
>
> ("The Landscape," *New and Selected Poems*, p. 131)

Keeping the door open, allowing the heart to learn about fullness and ache, is no easy task. It requires "letting in," permitting a vulnerability that licenses others to assert their will, for better or worse. I have placed myself nakedly before others and been told that all that I am was not enough and, at other times, been told to come closer. It is the coming closer that matters:

> *Tell your lovers the world*
> *robs us in so many ways*
> *that a caress is your way*
> *of taking something back.*
>
> ("Some Things I Wanted to Say to You,"
> *New and Selected Poems*, pp. 21–22)

With caresses, both literal and figurative, I take back what the world yanks away. With caresses, my hands learn what softness means, my eyes understand what it is to see, and my body discovers how to melt into another. Caressing, I am most fully human. With Dunn, I seek a way to move on, a way to live with promise:

> *Listen, my truest love, I've tried*
> *to clear a late-century place for us*

in among the shards. Lie down,
tell me what else you need.
Here is where loveliness can live
With failure, and nothing's complete.
I love how we go on.

("Loves," *New and Selected Poems*, p. 287)

Among the shards, always aware that I might fail, always knowing I must do more, I go on, searching for those places where "loveliness can live." To find such places, I must query, "tell me what else you need." Such a query offers a beginning, a starting place for connection. It is the only way I know to discover what I need. It provides me with what I want: "After the power to choose / a man wants the power to erase" ("What Men Want," *What Goes On: Selected and New Poems 1995–2009*, p. 195).

With Dunn's instruction, then, I end my remarks with an apology, an apology to all those who I have failed to ask to "tell me what else you need," failed to be the person I should have been, failed to stay present, failed to keep the poetry of their life in my life. It has been my loss, but I am thankful for this occasion to say, borrowing once again from Dunn, what I should have said before:

From the start all I wanted to explain
was how things go wrong,
how the heart's an empty place
until it is filled,
and how the darkness is forever waiting
for its chance.

("Instead of You," *New and Selected Poems*, p. 91)

Part I\

Listening to Myself and Others

Leaning in entails a deep listening, an ability to take in, an absorption. It calls for an individual's readiness and desire, depends upon that individual to be aware of his or her own situatedness, predilections, and behaviors. Part 2 is my attempt to do a deep listening, to lean into myself and others in the hope of coming to a better understanding. The section is built on the premise that I am a limited relational partner unless I have some insight into myself and unless I reach out to others. I seek a productive reflexivity that allows me to locate my limitations, to contemplate change, to become a better person. I want to be the attentive listener, the person who tries to hear what others are saying, who can take others' perspectives, who is quick to turn to the empathic gesture.

"Self-Portrait: Standing on a Nail," the first chapter in this section, is a cycle of fourteen sonnets I've written as an examination of my own way of moving through the world. The sonnets are my "persistent and compelling need … to give an account" of myself (Barrett, 2009, p. 93). Each sonnet can be read as a single line in the larger poem that might be seen as one overall sonnet with the final two sonnets functioning as the closing couplet. I borrow from the poetic tradition of using sonnet cycles to express love in order to show that my critical posture in the poem is, ironically, an act of self-maintenance, of self-caring.

Chapters 7, 8, and 9 are my efforts to understand others, to see if I can come to a satisfactory cognitive and affective engagement. By satisfactory, I mean an understanding that would gather consent, have resonance for those involved. I know I will never have complete understanding, but I might, as the ethnomethodologist Harold Garfinkel (1967) suggests, gather in enough of the other that we can move forward as if understanding has taken place. Chapter 7, "Reading Barthes as a Lover," and chapter 8, "Walking and Writing with Laurel Richardson: A Story in Poems," are gatherings. I select Barthes and Richardson, both well-known scholarly figures, so readers of these chapters can not only witness my leaning in, but also can hold up their own readings of Barthes and Richardson against mine. Chapter 9, "Three Tales of Understanding," builds upon limited knowledge I had about several acquaintances. I took as my task an imaginative leap, a construction of possible narratives. In this speculative inquiry, I tell each tale from a different narrative stance to put on display how one might stand in relationship to another, how leaning in takes many forms.

Chapter 6
Self-Portrait
Standing on a Nail

You are everyman, born in privilege
in the land of haves if you happen
to be the right race with money rolling
in, if you don't much mind a few little
inconveniences now and then, if you
don't much mind giving a little here and
there to ease the guilt you'd rather not keep,
if you don't much mind just staying where you'll
be secure. Having tossed, without much thought,
more than most will ever possess, having
more clothes in your walk-in closet than you'll
ever wear, having more than you can list,
you arise, ready to greet the day; it's
yours for the taking and you often do.

You are everyman, straight, filled with desire,
happy with your safe opposite, how it's
all laid out for you, all designed for you.
Wherever you look, one man, one woman.
It's all so convenient for you, you can,
without much cost, be supportive, open,
to those who aren't just like you. And you can,
without much risk, speak of the injustice,
sign a petition, march in a parade.
It's all so easy for you, no skin off
your bed, no fantasy denied, no soft
touch lost. So, you stand erect, proud, ready

to embrace the woman you love who knows
desire finds its way most fully in choice.

You are everyman, made of a little
of this and a little of that, none of
which is likely to give offense, none of
which separates you from the herd, none of
which will be held against you in a court
of your own laws. You get to speak on your
own behalf. You get to love who you wish.
You get to consume the world's resources
without pause, without conceding that they
may not be yours. You are a man who wants
and who is positioned to get. You are
invisible, everywhere, and deadly.
Your aim is to create more of your kind,
ones just like you, stupid and confident.

You are everyman, a father of two,
one who is your pride and toy, who you pull
out as if she were yours, as if you were
responsible, as if such showing let
everyone see just how wonderful you
are and one who you put away, as if
you were not responsible, as if excuses
on his behalf are enough to forgive
yourself. You are a son who got more than
he deserved and a brother who gives less
than he should; a husband who is still here,
still living in love, and still wanting to
do it right, believing as you do, that
our families are thick with blood and should.

You are everyman, a teacher by trade,
a licensing agent, nothing more, who
follows the rules, watching with care who is
to be let in and who must be kept out,
who, when looking into resistant faces,
longs to be home, reading what others find

boring, what others dismiss, who, on your
better days, believes and, on your worst, feels
exhausted, not only by those who fill
the empty chairs, but by those who have spent
too many years having others write down
what they have to say. Now, tumbling toward
the end, you still wonder if you were smart
enough or just cautious enough to last.

You are no man, seeing what you do see
and doing nothing, you who preach what needs
to be done and look away as if talk
is a sufficient cure, confession a
satisfactory action, as if these words
give you a pass. Forgive me, all, for I
have continued on, knowing. You, who think
such claims bring redemption, who move slowly
toward a never changing end, a quick-
sand that keeps everything in place, offer
platitudes for your own pleasure, propose
a politics of slogans where a heart
should be. You carry on, shameless, without
disturbing the world, assuming all is yours.

Fat and spoiled, you waddle along—you with
your hair growing thin, your feet sore, swollen,
your face cracked, speckled with dark moles and marks,
your ears sprouting unwanted hairs. You peek
at your penis below your belly, but
it's paltry, small as a retreating snail.
Your knees ache. Your back aches. Your neck is stiff.
You watch what you ingest, keep Tums near by.
You have your colonoscopy and take
your blood pressure with your daily pink pill.
Worried, you have five moles removed, tested.
You feel relieved, but watch as others grow.
Held together with medical glue, you
chew the future, rub your arthritic hands.

Fat and spoiled, you tilt your head to listen.
Nosy as a search dog, you position
yourself so you can take in strangers, take
in more than they know, take in that Aunt May
was still in the hospital, this time so
sick, and who knew if she were going to
make it. You like getting glimpses, getting
what isn't yours. You like hearing their stories,
their way of making sense, their slow and hard
rhythms. You like having without having
any obligation, assessing them
and feeling superior, consuming
them as if they were your appetizer,
your tidbit, there for your hungry pleasures.

Fat and spoiled, you drink a quick beer or two,
meet others who act just like you. You want
them to like you. Who doesn't? Who can live
alone? So, you buy overpriced candy
from their kids, send cards in times of sorrow,
play a round of golf or two. Talk settles
on sports, safe politics, and the weather.
You avoid religion as you would a
burning cross. You chat on chance encounters,
but no trips together, no secrets shared.
You complain together about work.
You listen half hearing, speak half caring.
And when troubles come, you do what you can
unless, of course, to do demands too much.

Fat and spoiled, you always want more, want more
attention, notice. You look for applause,
compliments, even from those you do not
know. You move to the center, cautious, not
wanting to overplay your hand. You wouldn't
want anyone to think you're self-centered,
wouldn't want anyone to think you're taking
too much, asking for too much, getting too
much. How crass it would be, you think, to seek

awards, honors or ceremonies in
your name, but you want the praise, you want it
all, need it so you can convince yourself
you're worthy, more than just another of
earth's parasites, taking more than you should.

Fat and spoiled, you thought it must be your right,
thought you were entitled to break a pledge,
an oath, that promises only mattered
if they didn't interfere with what you
selfishly wanted, that feeding, stroking
your little ego was permissible,
that no one would be hurt. You put yourself
first, put yourself into regret, put her
questioning how long the stink would last, how
to trust again, believe a word you said.
You wish to forget, turn away, erase.
Remorseful, you wish for absolution,
but betrayal sits, silent, holding on,
a reminder of what you once could be.

Fat and spoiled, you remember younger days,
when your body, tall and lean, had control,
could move into a swing, become taut, tight
as a coil, when the days seemed long and yours,
when you muscled in, claiming space, claiming
you had answers, when allies came and went
and lovers satisfied your needs. You were
on the make, making yourself into you,
making believe you were something, someone
who mattered. Now you smell of history
and when all is said and done, not much will
be said and much less done. You poke, dig in
your perfect ruins, an archeologist
with a shovel full, still searching for more.

In the end, how very easy to write
such tripe, to give the negative critique,
the self-portrait in lines masquerading
as raw truth, to let your own finger point

*at yourself—you know so well the faults, know
so well what you are willing to admit, know
the consequences, the potential fallout.
You've calculated it all, figured you'd
come out on top, that sympathy would come
for a man who tries, who is willing to
question himself, slap himself on behalf
of those who should. But, you're such a tricky
man, confessing with enough distortions
to permit the petty stories you tell.*

*In the end, your words ache with arrogance
Smug, you sit back convinced you have covered
your bases, that you are safe, still likeable.
You even think by admitting to your
arrogance, you somehow escape the charge.
You assume readers will be generous,
will ponder your complexity, will see
themselves written in your own human tale.
Yet, you finish feeling empty, sorry
for yourself, puzzled, wondering how you
might evolve. You see yourself still standing
on a nail, not knowing which way to move,
which way to lean, without causing more pain.*

Chapter 7
Reading Barthes
as a /over

> With the writer of bliss (and his reader) begins the untenable text, the impossible text. This text is outside pleasure, outside criticism, *unless it is reached through another text of bliss*: You cannot speak 'on' such a text, you can only speak 'in' it, *in its fashion*, enter into a desperate plagiarism, hysterically affirm the void of bliss (and no longer obsessively repeat the letter of pleasure).
>
> Roland Barthes, *The Pleasure of the Text*, p. 22

Entering

I seek a plagiarism of elegance, a desperate articulation of what cannot be held. I want to leave myself behind, to trust in the possibilities, to return again, new. I search for the moment of immersion when my body hums of a vibrant presence, when another enters whole, or should I say, when we enter together, forgetting our own elusive terms. It is an act of mimicry, a grammar filled with gratitude. Its place is between. There are no readers without writers, no writers without readers. I seek the salvation of surrender, the power of holding fingers to the pulse, the slippery bliss of encounter.

I begin by taking the text into my hands, feeling its slick, yellow-gold cover. I slid it first from a shelf, separated it from the others, turned it into a personal possession. I carried it home, eager to see what I now owned. It is thin as a whisper. It is cool, contained, bound like a foot in a leather shoe, measured as carefully as a tailored suit. I imagine it will be a good fit. On the front, it letters its introduction in brown and black, noting author, title, and translator.

On its back is a Susan Sontag quote. Two words stick: "histri-onic seduction," and I know immediately why the author of *Against Interpretation* might write in its behalf. It is no surprise that she would applaud the playful, the pleasurable text. It is no surprise that the person who wrote, "In the place of a hermeneutics we need an erotics of art" (p. 14), would find Barthes to her liking. It is no surprise that the person who wrote, "Art is seduction, not rape" (p. 22), would welcome Barthes's advances.

I also see his pictured smile, perhaps posed, his head tilting slightly to the side, his bright eyes challenging the camera's fixity, his gray hair neat as his tie. In the background are books whose titles were blurred by the camera's work, and to his side, a short biography that cannot be changed: born 1915—died 1980. His look denies such closure. Yet, his bright eyes will not let me go on without another reading. Those bright eyes, curved down like orange slices, carry a sadness, a recognition of the futility of it all, a realization of the empty efforts of words. I read fate.

Cupping its spine in my hand, I turn to its first pages. It tries to shut, to keep its secrets. I gently bend it back into my liking. It cracks like a bone finding its right place. I thumb its pages and discover its length (six-ty-seven pages), its generous spacing, its margins. We begin to settle in, together, almost comfortable, but tentative as one might hold a stranger's child. I turn to page one—simple, clean—*The Pleasure of the Text*, writ-ten a third of the way down from the top, separated like a little poem into two lines, the break, not surprisingly, following "pleasure." I turn again and meet a list of twenty-two titles under the heading, "Books by Roland Barthes." I know only five. At best, I will be a tourist on a short excursion, fumbling through streets and alleyways, trying to find my bearings in a city I will never be able to claim.

Named again are the author, title, and translator and the promise of a note by Richard Howard. Next, I see that I've found it long after its 1973 birth in another tongue, long after others have held it in their hands. I remember our first meeting years ago, read poorly when we all were first listening to the French, afraid of what we might learn. Now, I read its twentieth printing. The twentieth must surely signify Farrar,

Straus and Giroux's poor estimation of their own wisdom. It must surely say that history bears repeating. It must surely mean that many others have found the pleasure of his text.

I have read and heard others celebrate its pleasure, but I need to discover it for myself. I need to become present, to become the reader I am supposed to be—attentive, appreciative, and perhaps a bit confused. And when confusion comes, I need to accept it as my failure, my inability to see what is before me. I need to struggle. I need to be open, ready for the text to take its hold, to claim me as a prodigal son who has finally come home. I need to believe in the possibilities of pleasure, of bliss.

I need to read like a lover.

Rhythm

With pencil in hand, I begin in anticipation of what is to be found. I'm ready to underline, mark, and star, ready to use my system to note significance. I am poised. My breathing is shallow as if I were frightened in the night, listening. I want to know what is there, to put myself at ease, to take control. For my desire is the comfort of recognition, of stable categories that allow everything to settle securely into place, into the familiar. I wish to name its genealogy, its historical predecessors, its chronological order. I long for its summary paragraph, filed away but available for use should an appropriate occasion arise. Put in its place, it is mine to do with as I please. I want the pleasure of its bondage.

No, I want to give myself over, to welcome the intruder, to strip myself of protective garments. I wait for an invasion of sensibilities, a violent trespass, trembling forward, feeling its way in the dark. I'm looking for who will establish the rules, who will take charge and give commands. I breathe more quickly wanting to be entered, wanting to discover what I have not known. There are no safe words—only the penetrating violation. Perhaps I say more than I should, say more, being intimidated by the Father, than I believe, say more than I doubt.

So I begin. My initial steps are hesitant, flat-footed, awkward. Cautiously, we start our first dance without touching, facing each other, observing what the other can do. We want to know if we might dance at all, if our styles might come together, if our skills are equal to the task. At times we salsa, taking quick steps, side steps, a turning of backs, connecting again in hot sauce. At times we tap, take the stage to pound out our own beat, to show what we can do. At times we tango, filled with its drama. Staring together into the void, we move cheek to cheek. At times, we are line dancing, kicking up the dust, clapping together at just the right moment, stepping in unison to a rhythm everyone can find. At times, we settle into a waltz—I do not know if I lead or follow but we move together as if on air, as if nothing could stop us except our own desires.

We dance a painter's canvas. I notice a moment here. I get a glimpse there. I try to see it all. I change positions so that I might take it all in, so that I might see better. I rest at predictable places. Sometimes clear and sometimes blurred, my focus is pulled to specific spots and stops. I move around trying to settle in. I study, puzzle. I get excited. I yawn. I ponder. Points of clarity emerge on the underside of confusion, pushing obscurity away with letters, words, phrases, sentences, paragraphs, and page after sweet page.

Letters lick their lazy way, lounging around in groups, in pools of resonance. I know them by name, by sound. I get hooked on the fisherman's "J." I nail myself to Christ's "t." I listen for the noise of my own "I." They move in rows across the page, from left to right, leaving little gaps between. They swirl, curl, twist this way and that and are recognized for what they are: eardrops calling me out, calling me forward, calling me to words.

Words slide into me and point to "pleasure," to "bliss," and to the "erotic," and in their naming call forward a place to dwell, a sumptuous hall with all the appropriate appointments. I enter, pleased to be there, pleased to see what is before me, pleased to have been invited to this room. I see that there is enough space for me. I try to respect the host, adopting his tone, mimicking his manner, assuming his posture. Soon, we speak the same words. We point, saying there, and there, and there until we can toast each other in phrases.

Phrases wink a welcome, working the tongue into understanding, stringing words together like beads, round, connected by a thin line, fragile but ready to sustain itself, resistant to an unwanted pull. Sometimes prepositional, sometimes adverbial, but always doing nouns' work: naming, remembering beyond time, corralling the parts until they circle, like wagons, into sentences.

Sentences surround, claiming they are complete. One thought. One moment's utterance. One assertion, even when marked by a question. Here is a favorite: "The text is (should be) that uninhibited person who shows his behind to the Political Father" (p. 53). That sentence is so good in fact that it resists joining with others, that it refuses to settle in among others of its kind, that it shows the paragraph, that Political Father, its behind.

Paragraphs, trying to contain, huff and puff as they squeeze arguments into a ball. Paragraphs push and pull this way and that, indented to say, "This is new." Collecting sentences as a stamp collector would collect stamps, it puts things in order, has its reasons, knows its logic. Designed to please, it decides upon its viscosity, its stability, its mass. It is an energy force, forcing some reckoning, often before the page is done.

Pages turn, one after another, in order, in sequence. They are arranged like obedient soldiers, all lined up, marching on, in single file, thin as a sword, anticipating review. Some advance always aware of their actions, their presentation of arms; some parade by, eager, but never looking back; some move only by command; some pass, sad, because they have given so much or so little. Numbered, they know their beginning and end.

I swallow it all in. I wallow in it and then I think I am there, reading to write, writing to read. I think I have it whole but, of course, I don't. The letters cannot snare me; the words cannot hold me. Phrases jump out of place, jumble. Sentences float by. Paragraphs slip away. Pages leak. There are no anchors. In the pointing, everything seems to slide away, everything seems slippery as wet soap. But I have known their lather, their cleansing power. I bathe in wonder, a wonder that finds its fullest expression in the quote that begins this essay.

The quote locates itself in the contrasts between pleasure and bliss, between the expressed and the ineffable, between distance and surrender, and between the ordinary and extraordinary. These contrasts shape this reader's struggle. They are everywhere, page after page, each time offering curious claims, subtle changes, frustrating confusions. They will not hold still. Just when I believe I can pin them down, they shake me loose, wrestle free of any easy three-count press. These untenable contrasts resist my tenacious grip but I maneuver, in and out, until I know them by feel. Our bodies intertwine. I move with the clouds of my convictions toward a sensuous celebration.

I celebrate writers of bliss whose texts are beyond pleasure. Their texts are "untenable." They cannot be held, maintained, or defended. Such texts are "impossible" because they are what they are: open possibilities, opportunities available upon passionate encounter. They will not settle into place, not even in the moments following pursuit. Their potential insists upon continual recognition. "What about this?" "What about this?" they repeat like a demanding child. They offer no easy formula, no simple logic, no quick summary. They want no principles or rules to follow. They resist closure like a wild animal fights against the cage. They strive on instincts as they move across their terrain exposing their nature. They desire an erotics of now. They need no defenders.

With the impossible text frustration comes. I am disoriented, denied safe summary. What seems nailed shut springs open. What seems tightly tied unravels. I pore over passages, holding one line against another, writing in the margins, questioning what seems to slip away. Sometimes, there is no understanding. Sometimes, there is an understanding for the concentrated time of reading. Sometimes, understandings are too plentiful, too contradictory. I underline, take notes, re-read. I throw the book against the wall and then retrieve it for another try. It remains elusive. I blame it; I blame the translator; I blame myself.

Then, unexpectedly, a settling quiet comes, a private calm that allows me to accept what might be there. My desire for answers, my frustration, dissipates. I give myself permission to just listen. Only then do I begin to see. It is as if I have been placed within a magical garden, a never-ending maze with no entrance and no exit where I can stroll endlessly with my eyes wide open, without fear that I might not see everything there is to see or name everything that is there. It is a garden maze where the flower's beauty is in its complexity, its multiple folds.

To celebrate what cannot be held I must be content with productive ambiguity, an ambiguity whose various threads weave patterns appealing to the eye, to the touch. Such threads compliment and contrast one another as they stitch together their propositions, their passions, and their prayers. Such threads are not too loose, blowing aimlessly in the wind, nor too tight, so twisted and knotted that no one can sense what might be there. Productive ambiguity points to the needle's careful work. To celebrate what I cannot hold I must understand that the needle's work is to create a design that is never done.

To celebrate what cannot be held may just mean that the notion of productive needs to be shaken loose from any cognitive sensibilities. Perhaps the most productive is a place where there are no threads to follow or patterns to trace. In such a place, the productive produces more than what can be measured, more than a written formula, more than any mathematical equation. In such a place, the productive stuffs science down its pants and becomes a reproductive sensorium: a wet, slippery erotics, an intercourse of feelings. In such a place, the ineffable resides.

I celebrate writers of bliss whose texts speak the unspeakable, say the unsayable. This oxymoron, this possibility of saying what cannot be said, is an opportunity to stand within a world that cannot be, a world where the subjunctive turns into the declarative and the declarative into the subjunctive. It is a world where no one speaks so that everyone can hear what is being said. It is a world of guessing and gasping. I wander around, searching, touching the untouchable. I am an off-duty police officer, wiping away my fingerprints. I am an undertaker, burying what needs to be laid to rest. I am a guest entering the master bedroom. I am a lover.

Blissful texts prefer lovemaking to describing what lovemaking might mean. They are "outside criticism," outside the pleasure of my control. They do not bend to my words, do not succumb to my desires. They cannot be paraphrased, reduced, or revealed once and for all. They will not listen. Instead, they speak like poems, in whispers, in winks, in wishes. They mold my desires in their own image, making me speak in their own tongue.

I celebrate writers of bliss whose texts invite my blissful surrender. I read until I am present in my absence. I read toward a vigorous void, emptying myself, letting the text happen to me. I give myself over in order to be filled. I read myself into the text until I can no longer be found. I turn into a "desperate plagiarist." I speak only in its language, only in its spirit. Body joins body. There is no distance as blissful text meets blissful text. Such a union is an empathic seduction, a coming together: fingertips connect, hands caress, bodies curve into one another. Such a union is the lip's loving license. For this is the tongue's tale, told together, "hysterically," using the same speech, the same voice, in jubilant harmony.

Here is my attempt to reach Barthes with my own text of bliss, to take his quote and speak, "not 'on'" it, but "'in' it, *in its fashion.*" The critic in me feels that such an attempt is presumptuous, an arrogant and audacious act. How can I be so vain as to think that I might write in Barthes's fashion? How could I have such unwarranted hubris? Because I come not as a critic but as a poet writing love sonnets. Perhaps I write poor poems, technically flawed, trite, with forced rhyme. Perhaps I delude myself when I say I might speak as a poet. Perhaps I do not even know what a poem is. But I write as all poets do: I write with passion, with conviction, in the hope of transcendence. I write in faith that my efforts matter.

And I believe that all such efforts to reach beyond ourselves matter because without them we lose contact with our humanity, with who we are and who we can be. Such efforts matter because they are our best chance to leave our critical stances, our fortresses, to open our lives to other views and to embrace our enemies. This idealistic belief comes from a humanist's heart, a heart hardened against the possibility that life might be some other way. In short, such efforts matter because they are our best chance for connection and change.

I celebrate writers of bliss whose texts work against the ordinary, against the rusted results of routines. Such texts resist repetition, a repeating of the same old logics, even when those logics provide some comfort. They release what has been oppressed and suppressed in expression. I stand before them nodding an ecstatic "yes" to a world I have never seen. I am given new visions, variations for contemplation. I begin to see imaginative reorderings, alternatives to stagnant habits. They come like apparitions, like revelations, like gifts. I celebrate a politics of change, violent as words that slide beyond was and will.

But the critic in me returns asking if my celebration is justified, wondering if I am nothing but an old, deluded humanist, questioning if I have just been taught to think that such a celebration is possible when indeed there is no basis for my joy. I know these suspicions. In response I have nothing but memories of how Barthes's quote excited me, agitated me, took me beyond simple pleasure. He wrote me into bliss; I read him into bliss. I celebrate with Barthes because his words write the real, his words chart the possible, his words name the unnamable. I try to speak "in his fashion" because I've felt its power. I try because it is the right thing to do. I try because to do so is to see the world again.

I live in translation, not the Richard Miller translation from French to English, but the translation Barthes offers: a chance to move between his writing and our reading, between his assertions and our insertions, between Barthes's body and our own so that we might be transformed. Such is Barthes's invitation. He persuades us to become blissful readers. He puts his work forward like succulent fruit, ready to drip down our chins with our first full bites, nourishing us, filling us, until we feel stronger than before. It cleanses, freshens the mouth so that we might speak more clearly. We may note a bruised spot here or there, but we can cut it from the whole and leave it behind. Some parts may not come to the tongue as well as others but none spoils the overall taste.

I remember Barthes's response to his question, "What is significance?" He gives a simple but remarkable answer: "It is meaning, *insofar as it is sensually produced*" (p.61). Barthes offers the "sensually produced." He writes the erotic, turns me into his voyeur, always trying to see more. Through the keyhole he bored, I peer. I am aroused by quick glimpses and by long lingering perusals. I focus on what pleases me most, perhaps turning it into my fetish. I fixate upon it in my obsessive devotion. It controls my thinking, my way of moving through the world. I become its exhibitionist, showing it wherever and whenever I can. I pull it out in conversation; I fool with it while I'm writing. I am its pimp.

Exiting

I withdraw, pull back to see what and who I leave there. I look down and see letters, words, phrases, paragraphs, and pages, bound together under their yellow-gold cover. They matter. I also see the holes they leave, and they matter, too. What is said and what is left unsaid spread out before me. They are there for the taking, vulnerable, open as a deep wound. I fan the pages and glance at my own markings—underlines, stars, scribbles, and quibbles—a palimpsest of my own desires, neatly and respectfully rendered. Soon, I will pull myself away. But first, I will stroke it as one might caress a lover who is now welcoming sleep. It will be a moment of loving sadness, a moment of thanks. Then, slowly, I will turn away, carefully, so as not to disturb, and I will not forget.

I also see Barthes or who I want to call Barthes. There he is, smiling, satisfied with what I've done. He knows about our time together, the difficulties, the pleasures, the bliss. He knows of the collapse of our communication, the sorrow of our sociology, the haze of our history. Yet, he is still there. I feel his humid air, still, surrounding me. I feel its thick moisture lick its strange seduction. Look, he is coming back to me, knowing what we had, knowing how our muscles loosen in the heat.

And I see my reflection, my curious other self who is no longer the same. Maybe my other self needed Barthes, needed him now, and in such need, perverted him to fulfill my desires. Maybe Barthes is my beautiful and bestial fiction. Maybe I only see myself. What I do know is that as I look at my reflection, I see how I have changed. I am a different reader, one who wants to redefine what connection might mean, one who wants to write in bliss, in a poetics of response. I long for a new space, a place to be rather than a place to see. And in such a longing, maybe, for just one single, impossible moment, I am Barthes.

Chapter 8
Walking and Writing With Laurel Richardson
A Story in Poems

This essay, a tribute to Laurel Richardson's work, is composed of a collection of poems that respond to her own call for and use of the poetic in sociological and ethnographic research. The piece is divided into four sections, Poeticizing Theory, Poems on Academic Life, Love Poems, and Poems of Evaluation, each with the intent of employing poetry as a "creative analytic practice." I lean in, trying to move toward Richardson, trying to understand, trying to step in her steps.

> If the goal of ethnography is to retell 'lived experience,' to make another world accessible to the reader, then, I submit that the lyric poem, and particularly a sequence of lyric poems with an implied narrative, comes closer to achieving that goal than other forms of ethnographic writing.
>
> (Richardson, 1997, p. 180)

Part 1: Poeticizing Theory

Lived Experience: Quote to Poem

(Writing Story: The following poem combines a quote from Richardson and a poetic elaboration. Each column can be read down and each line can be read across.)

> Lived experience .... that sweet fruit
> is lived in the body, ... is taken, taken in, whole and ripe,
> and poetic representation .... picked and pushed to perfection,
> can touch us where we live, ... making
> in our bodies .... the grape's last offering.
>
> (Richardson, 1997, p. 143)

A Poetic Meditation

Instead of 'going into' the field, we might embark on a 'pilgrimage' or imagine ourselves 'walking with' people. In 'walking with' we are embodied, self-consciously reflexive, partial knowers, conveners, ministers,—not 'insiders' or 'outsiders.'

(Richardson, 1997, p. 185)

The journey is always long, even when there are few miles to travel. There must be the time to see and hear, the opportunity to take in, the willingness to feel. You may become tried, exhausted as an old mule at the end of a long trail. You may think that you'll just give up. But remember, it doesn't just happen; it doesn't just come. One slow step after another. Stay alert. Watch where you are stepping. Many dangers exist. But, if you can place your foot just the right way at just the right time, then that one step can change you, change you forever. You will find yourself spinning while standing perfectly still. You will see yourself staring into the previously unseen. You will meet yourself and you will leave yourself behind. And, you will know for the first time that you do not know what you must. You will realize that you will never know. And you will know that you have no other choice than to keep on. That is life's ritual and life's demand. Your search is for the sacred, human walking with human, open, trying.

Crystallization: A Poetic Plea

In postmodern mixed genre texts, the writers do not triangulate; they crystallize. There are far more than 'three sides' by which to approach the world.

(Richardson, 1997, p. 92)

Again

Tell it again
and again,
tell it so that all
hear and all
are heard,
tell it so many times
that we know
there is always more
to tell,

tell it so that light
pours through,
a prismatic light,
a rainbow
of desire.

Tell it
again
to be fair.
Tell it enough
times to learn who
we are.
Tell it again
so we know
what to do.

Tell it
again and again
straight as
arrows
one after another
from all directions
crisscrossing,
shooting
for
the heart.

Creative Analytic Practice: Investigative Poetry

(Writing Story: I borrow the term "investigative poetry" from Ed Sanders [1976] who argues that poetry, with its ability to penetrate a subject, is particularly well suited to do the work of history. Sanders's ideas are very much in keeping with Richardson's [1999; 2000b] thoughts on creative analytic practices.)

Permission from the Heart

Let the poem speak in places where it has been forbidden,
Let it come forward singing songs of the sadly forgotten,
Let it write the heart before the heart shrivels, famished.

Let it seep, slowly, into the pores and settle like crazy jazz,
Let it probe, deeply, into the tissues and pull apart the joints,
Let it flow, forever, to and from the heart in juicy justice.

Let it uncover the feel of things in the lick of language,
Let it leak the unspeakable, liberate our lonesome lives,
Let it heal us all in its lusty lines, in the heart's lessons.

Poetic Claims

Ethnography's ear is always bending, its eye always blinking, its touch always bewildered.

Ethnography's dance is joyous as long as it never stumbles in just one place, as long as it never stops seeing through the dust it stirs, as long as it never ends.

Ethnography's heart is exposed; it is inappropriate, vulgar, and essential.

Ethnography's purpose is to connect, to tie a rope around the researcher's neck.

Ethnography's body bleeds.

Part 2: Poems on Academic Life

The University: A Dramatic Monologue

Finding a Place

It wasn't what I expected.
I imagined a place where minds
could share, explore,
be with each other,
where ideas could nestle
next to different ideas
without anyone taking exception,
where talk could move
to the body
like a healing ointment.

Instead, I found their tongues
slapping my face,
their bites
scarring my back,
their hearts
hiding.
It wasn't how
I wanted to be.

I had to find a sanctuary,
a woman's space,
sacred,
where in comfort I could be
as vulnerable and strong
as an open hand,
where my daily work could sing
of human life,
connecting,
dancing,
spine to spine
fingers locked
in our ritual
of defiance
and joy.

Mind/Body

How valid can the knowledge of a floating head be?

(Richardson, 1997, p. 167)

The Floating Head

He enters without bothering to acknowledge anyone
except himself, places his notes on the lectern, and begins.
He speaks in heavy tones and with a furrowed brow.
His work is serious business, important, and
dare he say it, the Truth. He has no doubt. He
has figured it all out. He has asked all the right questions,
run all the numbers, examined all the angles
he considers relevant. He knows what is what. He

goes on and on, eating more than the hour, confidant
all recognize the profundity of his remarks. He
trusts that his arguments will be tomorrow's quotes.
His logic, he can't help but believe, will prove it all.
Satisfied with the gifts he gives, he sits and nods
to polite applause. Pearls for swine, he thinks.
He accounts for their blank stares by believing that
only he and his colleagues understand scientific rigor. He
repeats this enterprise, year after year, swelling
with the enormity of his own significance, until one day,
he noticed, somewhat to his surprise, that he had left
in the lecture hall his own body squirming on the floor.

The Feeling Body

She enters, afraid but committed to tell all
she knows, fumbles with her papers, and moves
in front of the lectern. She smiles at all who
have gathered and then a sad seriousness crosses
her face. She begins a story of lives in pain,
lives hurt by our indifference, lives suffering
from our injustices. At times, she cannot go on.
She closes her eyes and sees too much. She worries
that no one will understand, that no one will do
anything. After talking longer than she expected,
she hardly hears the loud applause. I failed,
she thinks, I should have said many other things.
But person after person approaches her and offers
tender thanks. She allows herself some hope. Then,
proof: A woman, somewhat disheveled, slowly
comes forward. So sorry to bother you, she says,
but you were talking about me. You were telling
everyone about my life. Her tears were falling
faster than her words. They embrace, body to body,
and after everyone else has left the room, they leave
together, arm in arm, making sure the other is okay.

Lines of Plagiarized Possession: An Idiosyncratic Reading

(Writing story: The following poem is composed primarily of lines from two sources from Richardson's [1997, pp. 183, 186-87; 2000a] work. In both pieces, books are used as powerful metaphors for larger points. In this poem, however, I knowingly misread Richardson's essays to demonstrate how her language possessed me in a manner different from, but perhaps not altogether removed from, her intent.)

Books

Finished bookcases,
clean, white planks,
waiting
like a tabula rasa
for order.

I love touching them, classifying them,
alphabetically, chronologically, topically,
by color, size, favorites,
ideologically—
Parson's to the right,
Marx to the left.

All of my books—
hundreds and hundreds—
communication, performance, gender,
theory, philosophy, methods,
writing guides, ethnographies, poetry,
essays, fiction, art.
My books—my life?

I will I define myself.
I will place them on shelves.

Part 3: Love Poems

(Writing story: The poems in this section spin off of Richardson's [1997] poems about Louisa May, about her own life, and about marriage and the family. The poems, then, could be described with what Alexander [2000] calls the "generative story," Smith [1998] identifies as the "Canterbury Effect," and Heaton [1998] designates as "cannibalistic.")

Two Poems Based Upon Imaginary Interviews

Louisa May Revisited

I knew I had rattled on
for just too long,
but I can't imagine why
what I said—
what we said—
caused such an uproar.
How did you manage
to get through all that
controversy?

I thought how you talked
about me was just fine.
I know you skipped some things
but you couldn't say
every single thing I said
and I like how you did me—
you even did my Tennessee accent.
And what was all that nonsense
about the original me?
Did they think I just live
on paper?
I'm as valid as anyone.
And how funny they thought
that you were me!
I just don't know why
those men were so upset.
After all, you got
what I said

and I just live
a normal sort of life.

I glad you got it all
written down.
Someday, I want Jody May
to read it so she'll know
why I told you
our story.
John, too, should read it.
I don't think the poor man
has ever figured out
why I'm happy to have him
around for Jody May,
just not for me,
just not in that kind of way.

I guess just about everything
that could be said
has been said by now.

That's the way that worked out.

John's Turn

I know this really isn't about me
and I want to respect that
but I also want to say
how I see things.

I don't think Louisa May
should have been talking
about our private affairs.
She might think everything
in her life is normal,
but that's not how I see it.
It isn't right
that she keeps me
connected the way she does.
Don't get me wrong.
I want to be there—

I love Jody May
and I have to admit,
I love Louisa May too.
I just think it's strange how
she's set things up,
me being a part of everything
but not really a part
and even stranger
that she would tell everybody
about it.
I think it's odd,
real odd.
But she won't have it
any other way.
She repeats that line of her's—
that's the way that worked out.
It drives me crazy.
There is no talking to her about this
and, if you ask me,
there should be no talking
to strangers either.

A Found Poem

Vespers

Uncle Jack's daughter, Lilly
gave birth to a fifth son.
He was blind and armless
and his heart was outside
his chest.
She named him Jack
and buried him
next to her father.

Aunt Gertrude,
partially submerged
in their claw-footed bathtub,
was crying.
There was blood.

Mother came in and out
tending to her.
An abortion.
Father took me home.

(Richardson, 1997, p. 223)

Three Poems: Marriage and the Family

Taking Her to the Vet

She's something, Doctor.
She's so picky.
Seldom eats everything
on her plate.
Always grooming herself,
secretive,
staring off into space.
Then, she'll want to snuggle
and I can hardly move,
but if I approach her,
she hisses and moves away.
And those claws—
you never know when
she might use them.
At night, if I'm snoring,
she'll get out of bed
and sit in front of the TV.
Is there anything, Doctor,
anything at all,
that can be done?

Being Married Is

taking a wishbone
before it's clean
offering a challenge

to years of things
unsaid, holding on,
hope against hope

knowing you must try
to win, pressing
thumb to thumb

as if a simple game
with its tricks, its threats,
its tragedy could tell

how bones break.

My Place

If I were a serving spoon
I would be available
when things are too hot
or could use some help
getting from here to there.
My deep bowl would hold
what is needed.
My handle, a convenience.
My design, a small comfort.
My weight, a constant.
When done, I would be forgotten,
left behind with the leftovers.
I would know my place.

Part 4: Poems of Evaluation

(Writing story: The following poem plays with Richardson's [2000b] evaluative criteria for assessing alternative modes of ethnographic representation. Her criteria ask if an essay made a substantive contribution, had aesthetic merit, created an impact, deployed reflexivity, and offered an expression of reality.)

Summary Poem Questioning Merit

Did It?

Did it get to you?
Did it?
Did it make you mad
Or glad?

Did it stir you up,
make you think,
make you want to act?
Did it?
Did it tap into the poem's power?
Did it say something
of value?
Did it contribute to the dialogue
in some meaningful way?
Did it matter?
Did it tell a story
you can trust,
a story that was fair?
Did it?
Did it question itself enough?
Did it turn back
and wonder if
this is authentic?
Did it?
Did it take in Richardson,
walk with her,
write with her?
Did it speak her name?
Did it?

A Cinquain Asking Forgiveness

At issue is not whether we should write narratives—we always do—
but how the stories we tell do and do not reinscribe tyrannies large and
small—do and do not improve material, symbolic, and aesthetic conditions of our lives.

(Richardson, 1997, p. 77)

Sorry

Sorry,
there should be more,
better, in step, closer,
clearer, like crystal, like a hand
blistered.

Chapter 9
Three Tales of Understanding

Tale One: Making It

I guess you want to know what I'm doing out here, sitting alone in this awful Motel 8. Well, last night, there we were, Mike and I, just sitting on the sofa, and he, of course, was watching one of his ball games. I was bored and I just wanted to make conversation. So I asked him: "How well do you think you know me?" and he gave me one of his grunt answers: "Good." He didn't even turn his head away from the game.

"What color are my eyes?" I went on, covering my eyes so he couldn't get a peek.

"I don't know. They're lots of colors," Mike says.

"Lots of colors? Like what?"

"Maybe some yellow. Some green."

"My eyes are hazel," I tell him, dropping my hands from my eyes. After eleven years you'd think he'd be able to do better than "maybe some yellow and some green."

"What kind of color is that?"

"That kind of color is the color of my eyes," I shot back. He didn't even bother to look. He just shrugged. So I pushed on: "What's my favorite holiday?"

"Maggie, I'm trying to watch the game," he says. "I don't want to play twenty questions."

"Just tell me what my favorite holiday is?"

"Christmas?"

"No, it's my birthday and for your information, my birthday is next Saturday."

"I know that," he says, but he only knew because I reminded him a few days before.

"I wouldn't have guessed that you did," I told him. I got up from the sofa, got in the car, and went to the mall without telling him another word. I thought I'd do some retail therapy, but I couldn't stop thinking about everything. Then it came to me clear as can be: unless things changed, I didn't want to be with Mike. I deserve more. I don't have to live like this, hating my life. I went home and fixed dinner. I decided I'd wait until dinner before bringing anything up.

"Things have to change between us," I start.

"What things?" Mike says, mixing his peas into his mashed potatoes.

"When was the last time you were happy?"

"When the Bears won," he says, missing the point.

"I mean, when was the last time you were happy with us," I say, trying my best to keep calm.

"I'm happy with us, except when you make a mountain out of nothing," he goes.

"I'm thinking of leaving you," I blurt out. I wanted him to know that I was serious, that it wasn't "nothing."

"Don't be ridiculous," he says, chewing on the bone of his pork chop. I hate when he does that. He starts going on and on about how I should feel grateful for all the things he does for me and how I expect too much because I've watched too many movies. Then he says it: "You get married, have kids, and then you die." He knows we can't have kids. As you know, Wendy, we tried—and he wouldn't consider adopting.

"Sometimes it doesn't work out that way," I tell him.

"Sometimes it doesn't," he says, still eating.

Neither one of us were saying a word. When the sound of his fork stopped scraping against his plate, I asked, "You finished?"

"Yeah, I'm done."

I cleared the table and did the dishes, but the whole time my mind was racing: Will this be how it will end? Is this it? Was it all about not being able to have kids? Hadn't we worked through that? I'm only thirty-three, I thought, I can still have kids if I want. Do I want out? What would I do? Where would I go?

He had gone into the family room and flipped on TV. I went in, took the flipper, and turned the TV off. "Do you think we can work things out?" I say.

"You tell me," he says.

"It's not just my choice."

"It seems like it is to me," he says, putting it all on me. Then, he reaches for the flipper and turns the TV back on.

I went upstairs, grabbed a few things, and came here. I don't want Mike to know where I am. You've got to promise, Wendy, you won't tell. I have to figure this out. I don't know what Mike is thinking. I don't know what he wants. I'm not sure what I want.

I don't know where Maggie is. She's never done anything like this before. I'd call her mother, but her mother would get worried. Maggie would be furious. I can't do that. She's gotten angry before, but never like this. She didn't come home last night.

I shouldn't have said anything about kids. It just slipped out. I was making a point: life isn't a big romantic fairytale. Most of it is routine. Having kids, I know Maggie's told you, is a touchy subject for us. I should have known better. After we found out I was the problem, things changed. Having kids meant a lot to Maggie. I let her down. Maggie thought we should adopt or go to a sperm bank or something. I just couldn't see it. If it wasn't ours, well, I just don't know. Don't get me wrong. It's great if people are comfortable doing that. But for me, it would be a reminder. Kids became one of those things we never discussed. Sometimes, we'd see some family with kids. We both think about it, but we never say a word. That's how we deal with it. I shouldn't have said anything.

I had a chance to coach a Little League team. I told Maggie. She says, "I thought they only let the kids' fathers do that."

"No. That doesn't matter," I told her.

"I'd think it would matter to you," she says. "Won't you just be wishing one of those kids was yours?"

I didn't answer her. Her remark made me think though. Maybe it would be too hard for me. For her, too. I turned it down. I should've done it. I've always loved kids. Maybe that would've helped. I enjoy my sister's kids, but I don't get to see them that often.

Things haven't been too good with us lately. We hardly ever make love. I guess she thought what's the point? And no matter what I do, it's wrong. If I take out the garbage, it's too soon or too late. If I eat everything on my plate, I eat like a pig. If I leave something, I don't like her cooking. She always makes it sound like it's a little joke. She just digs at me:

"Well, my little pig gobbled down everything on his plate, didn't he?" she'd say.

"It was good," I'd answer.

"That's why my little pig is turning into a little fat boy," she'd say. If I say anything, she says she's just teasing, that I need to lighten up.

We went to a marriage counselor. It was expensive. Our insurance wouldn't pay a dime. We weren't getting anything out of it—we would just repeat what we had already said at home. This counselor would just sit there, nodding his head. He'd ask if I understood what Maggie was saying. I understood. I heard it all before. I told Maggie I didn't want to go back. She was upset but she dropped it right away. I don't think she was getting much out of it either.

I don't know what I should do now. I've tried and tried her cell. No answer. If she doesn't come back soon, I'll call her mother. If I have to call the police, that's the first thing they ask. Call me, Wendy, if you hear anything. Please. If Maggie was in the hospital or something, they'd call. I could drive by her mom's. See if her car is there. If she is, what should I do? She doesn't want to talk to me. If I go out looking, I'll miss her if she comes back home.

When Maggie called me and told me she was staying at Motel 8, I was shocked. I knew they went through a rough time when they found out they couldn't have kids, but I thought things had settled down for them. They seemed happy. Just last week Bill and I had dinner with them. Everything seemed fine. I was surprised that Maggie didn't come straight over to our house if she were having trouble. I told her that but she said she didn't want Mike to know where she was. So she's staying at that creepy motel. I don't like her being there.

After I got home from talking with Maggie, Mike called. He was so worried. He asked me if I'd heard from Maggie but because I promised Maggie, I told him I hadn't. I hated lying to him. He was so upset. I never heard Mike ramble on and on like that. It's the first time I've heard his side of the story, and there's some truth in what he said. I've seen Maggie make fun of Mike, and sometimes it seemed to me she pushed too hard. I never said anything to Maggie about it, but I could tell it bothered Mike. Bill noticed it, too. Sometimes when just the two of us were together, she'd start talking about Mike's faults, say that he was boring, that all he liked to do was watch sports, that getting him to talk was like getting a drop of water in the desert. There have been times when I've seen Mike go a whole evening without hardly saying a word. He's not the most outgoing person you'll ever meet. But he's not a bad man. One day I told her she needed to start thinking about Mike's good qualities or she'd wake up one morning an old woman who hated her husband.

Bill says that no matter what, I shouldn't take sides—both of them are our friends. Our job, he says, is just to be there for them, to let them figure out what they want to do. I know Bill is right but I've been friends with Maggie long before Mike ever entered the picture. We're like twins.

Mike told me that they hated counseling. He's right. Maggie hated it too. The problem was the counselor they were seeing. I told Maggie I thought they needed to get a different counselor—everything she told me about him makes me think he doesn't know what he's doing—but she said that she thought counseling was too hard on Mike and that she thought she should let it go. I told her not to but she let it drop. I guess they never resolved their feelings about not being able to have kids. It's a shame that they aren't like Bill and me. We decided long ago that we didn't want any kids, and we never looked back. I guess some people aren't happy until they make little miniatures of themselves. Maybe that's why Mike never wanted to adopt. If he couldn't have a "Mini Mike," he didn't want any. I think they should have adopted; it would have been better for them. It could have worked out. How they left it, the problem just kept getting bigger and bigger. Maggie started resenting Mike, although she denied it, and Mike withdrew. Maggie would attack, and Mike would withdraw more.

I don't know what to tell either one of them. I love Maggie but I know she can be hard, expect too much, and Mike can just shut off. After they found out about not being able to have kids, he got worse and worse.

I did keep telling Mike that I was sure that Maggie was fine because I knew she was safe, even though I don't like where she is staying, and kept telling them both that I thought things would work out. I do—they both really love each other. The kid thing is just one of those life disappointments. They have too much together to just let it go. Maybe they would be happier if they just spilt up. Maybe they've reached a place where there is no going back, but I don't think so. I think they'll make it.

Tale Two: Taking Stock

You thought there'd be more but here you are, age forty-nine, about to cross the half-century mark, married for the second time with three kids, one from your first marriage and two from your current one, who seem happiest when you leave them alone, content as long as you give them money when they want it and the keys to the car, and soon two more of them will be off to college and you'll have their college tuition to pay that you wish you had saved for, but you don't know how that would've been possible, given what you make, and even counting what your wife brings in, there is never enough.

You thought there'd be more than the four bedroom house with mortgage payments beyond what you can afford and a lawn service that charges more than you think you should pay; the neighborhood that is nice, safe, but with neighbors who live inside closed doors and whose names you do not know, except for the one who lives right next door, who you just nod to when you see him; the church you attend, filled with hypocrites you can't abide, always with their hands out asking for more than the monthly check you always send, who think that they have a direct line to God, who think that only they know what the Bible means; and the city you live in with its outrageous taxes and few services, its mediocre chain restaurants that offer overpriced food without much taste, its traffic you'd only expect in a major city, and its corrupt officials from the police to the mayor who line their pockets with the citizens' hard earned money.

You thought there'd be more than Kiwanis on Wednesdays and wasting money on an occasional football or basketball game at the local college with a few guys you call your friends whose racist and sexist jokes trouble you, but who you let go on without saying a word; you who thought friends were people who would always be there, who you could count on, but who you now believe would walk away if troubles came, use them as they use you, to fill a few hours here and there, maybe have a laugh or two; you who thought you'd always have friends find yourself without a friend that matters, without someone you'd lend money, without someone you'd take in.

You thought there'd be more than giving nineteen years of your life to a company that hardly pays you what you think you're worth, that has stuck you right in the middle of the corporate ladder with little chance of moving up, that could go under or decide to relocate, leaving you without any prospects in a town of the unemployed and unemployable; more than dealing with an assistant who is only good enough to keep himself from getting fired but not good enough to take some of the load off your shoulders; more than working with other middle managers who think you're old school, out of ideas, a liability, who would stab you in the back if they thought it would advance their career.

You thought there'd be more after leaving your first wife for your second, after thinking you now knew what love was only to discover that after time the same flatness set in, the same routines, the same bills, the same diminished desires; and now, after investing twenty-one years, you, who always thought you could figure everything out, find yourself trying to decide if things could be better between the two of you, if you're locked into a relationship that is convenient but with little satisfaction, caught in the same old dance you danced once before, trapped into prolonged sadness.

You thought there'd be more, here on the cusp of your fiftieth birthday, wondering if this is your mid-life crisis, laughing at yourself, a cliché, mocking yourself, wanting to understand how everything brought you here, thinking that surely there must be more, more of everything, hoping to convince yourself that it all wasn't a waste, an expenditure that left you with nothing to hold on to, nothing to believe in, and nothing to say or do.

Tale Three: Burdens

After the doctor told Ellen she had breast cancer, she heard little else. She sensed that he was still talking, but his words seemed to her like an annoying hum, like the incessant noise of mosquitoes swarming around her. She was jolted back to him when he asked, "Do you have any questions?" but the best she could muster was "No." She found herself outside the medical center trying to remember where she had parked. She glanced down and saw she was holding an appointment slip—in one week she would see another doctor. A woman, dressed in a medical uniform, approached her. "Are you okay?" she asked. "Yes," Ellen managed. "I'm just trying to find my car." As Ellen spoke she saw it and started walking. The woman watched her for a moment and then went on her way.

Once in her car, Ellen glanced at the sun spreading across the dashboard and began to cry, first hard rushing tears, then deep sobs that shook her, then a quiet whimper. She reached for a Kleenex in her purse and began to gather herself. Those tears are what I needed, she thought. They're a release after living so long not knowing. Now I can deal with it. So many women have faced this. One in six was the statistic that came to her. And so many women have survived. It's not the death sentence it once was. She began to make a list of what she needed to do. First, she thought, I need to tell John. He's home, wanting to know. Just as quickly as she felt energized when she considered the tasks ahead, sadness pushed its way in. She didn't want to bring this news into their house, their marriage. It had been bad enough living with the uncertainty. What would the certainty do?

John heard the garage door squeak and was beside the car before Ellen had a chance to turn it off. "What did the doctor say?" he asked through Ellen's cracked window. The waiting for him had been unbearable.

Ellen had been preparing herself for her talk with John on the drive home, but she did not imagine it happening in the garage. "Give me a minute. I'll tell you everything I know," she began. "Let's get inside. I need some water."

"Okay. You want a glass of tap water or bottled? John asked. He was looking at her as they walked in, trying to read the news on her. He saw her red eyes and feared the worst.

"Bottled, please."

"You go sit down. I'll get the water." He returned shortly and asked again, "What did the doctor say?"

"I'll tell you but you have to stop looking at me like that."

"Like what?"

"Like I'm some alien creature or something," Ellen said and took a long drink of her water.

"Sorry. I'm just anxious to know what the doctor said," John replied, unaware that his look had been unsettling.

"The doctor said I have breast cancer."

"Oh," John said. "I'm so sorry, Ellen." He reached for her and tried to pull her to him. When she did not come, he let his arm drop from her shoulder and took her hand. John thought a hug would be what she would have wanted. He felt confused, uneasy. "We'll get through this," he added.

Ellen knew John was trying to be supportive but right now, to her surprise, he seemed like another problem. She was still processing. She didn't feel ready, despite thinking about what she'd say to John on the way home, to lead him through this. She wanted space.

"Can we talk about this later?" Ellen asked. "I'm just not ready to talk about it."

"Sure. I understand," John said.

Ellen almost laughed when she heard John's claim of understanding, but she held herself back and said: "I think I'd like to curl up on the sofa for a while."

"Sure. I understand," John repeated.

Ellen wrapped a throw around her and closed her eyes. Her mind was racing. Did John understand that soon he would have a wife with only one breast, perhaps none? Did John understand what was ahead for them? Did John understand that she might not be here in six months? After an hour or so, Ellen pulled herself up. She knew she had to answer John's questions. It was only fair to him.

"I go see a Dr. Meyers next week," Ellen said, picking up her appointment slip and reading his name. "He'll do the surgery."

John put down the book he was holding in his hands. He thought he'd read while Ellen slept but he found himself just looking at the words.

He wanted to know exactly what the doctor said. He wanted to know what was ahead for them both. When Ellen spoke, he came quickly to her side. "What will that involve?"

"My left breast. He's going to cut it off." John winced, and Ellen knew her words were too blunt.

"I mean, do you know how extensive the surgery will be?" John said, picking his words carefully.

"When I talk with Dr. Meyers," Ellen replied, trying to soften what she had said, "he'll make a recommendation about what he thinks should be done. I'll have some choice. It depends on how aggressive I want to be."

"What are you thinking?"

"I don't know. I want to hear what Dr. Meyers has to say."

"Are you sure you'll have to lose your breast?"

"Evidently my left breast has too many spots and there are some indications that it may have spread," Ellen reported. "Maybe it can be saved."

"We won't know anything final until you talk with Dr. Meyers. Right?" John said, wanting to sound hopeful, wanting to deny the facts.

"Well, we could get a second opinion."

"Do you want to do that?"

"I don't know, John," Ellen said, getting impatient with John's desire for answers. "I have a question for you," Ellen continued. "Are you ready for all of this?"

"What do you mean?" John was startled that their conversation had turned toward him.

"I mean, are you ready to face everything that is ahead for us? Are you ready for a wife without breasts?" Ellen shot back.

"I'll do whatever I can," John replied. Then he added, as he had before, "We'll get through this."

"I have to believe that," Ellen said. But she wasn't sure if John had answered her second question. She wondered most of all if he meant get through the surgery and the following treatment or if he was referencing their relationship. "And when I'm standing there, sick, without any hair, without any breasts, will you still love me?"

"Of course, I will," John said, but the image found a place deep inside John. It frightened him, and it would not dissolve.

Ellen leaned over and kissed John lightly on the lips. "Thank you for saying that." She realized that John could say little else, but she still wanted to hear those words. She also understood that John wouldn't know if their love would survive until they had gone through it all. "Keep telling me you love me, okay?"

"I will."

"Promise?"

"Promise."

"You've always been a boob man. What if I don't have any boobs?"

"First," John said, "we don't know if that is going to happen. Second, I'm an Ellen man, not a boob man. I'll love you no matter what. And third, even if they have to take a breast, they can make you another one."

"You make it sound like there's a boob-making assembly line," Ellen laughed.

"Yeah, there is this factory," John said, pleased that he made Ellen laugh, "where they make all sizes and shapes. Big ones. Little ones. You name it."

"Well, you'll have to help me pick out my next ones."

"Seriously," John said, "I do think reconstructive surgery is pretty routine. You can ask Dr....what's his name?"

"Meyers."

"Yeah, ask him. I think sometimes they can do it all in one operation."

Ellen felt that John was being helpful and sensed, too, that he liked being in that role. She could hear him gaining momentum, gathering confidence. I'll have to make sure, Ellen thought, that John always feels that way. And as she assigned herself that task, John came to her once again as a burden. Even when he wasn't helping, even when he was helping, she'd have to make him feel useful. The obligation tried to settle in but she resisted. She would not, could not, take it on. It was a time when she had to focus on what she needed, not what John needed.

"John, sometimes, as we are going through this, I might not be very nice to you. I'm not sure what I might do, but I know sometimes I'll have to focus just on me. Okay?"

"That's perfectly understandable," John said. "Don't worry about me." John was working to imagine how the life that he and Ellen knew might change. He felt disturbed, without control, and it made him uneasy.

"I do worry about you," Ellen said, "but, right now, I don't want to think about that. I have to direct all my energy to getting better."

"That's what I want you to do. I'll be fine."

"I think there are some support groups on the web. They might be helpful for both of us," Ellen offered. "And I know we can count on Lisa."

"And you can count on me," John said, hoping what he had just promised would be true.

That night in bed, John curled his body around Ellen's. He let his arm drape over her side and his hand cradle her breast. It felt good to hold her like this, John thought. Ellen, unable to sleep, wanted him there, holding her, and she wanted him to remove his hand, to move to his side of the bed.

Part III
Watching Men

"Watching Men" is about gender and sexuality, about how I, as a straight male, negotiate cultural scripts that lead me into and away from behaviors I enact with others. I lean, marked as a gendered and heterosexual person, trying to find a way of being that feels right to me. I want to resist adopting cultural dictates without stopping to reflect, without recognizing my responsibilities, without insisting upon agency. I want to consider what culture offers and to adopt a stance that manages power ethically and that settles into my body with comfort. When I do culture wrong, my desire is to question if that doing is productive or counter-productive for myself and others. In the three chapters that follow, I offer what I believe are productive permissions. Each in its own way pushes against culture's regulatory force. Each in its own way lets me entertain alternative ways of being.

In chapter 10, "Making My Masculine Body Behave," I locate my argument in the familiar notion that gender is a performed act. I borrow Constantin Stanislavski's vocabulary for creating a role for the aesthetic stage to show how my everyday performances of masculinity do and do not measure up to the dominant cultural ideal. I end by calling for a rewrite of the cultural script. "Jarheads, Girly Men, and the Pleasures of Violence," chapter 11, offers twenty short tales that link gender and violence. Some of the stories are based in specific incidences from my own life and others point to more general cultural practices that I participate in as a cultural member. I find myself most comfortable on the jarhead/

girly man continuum when I am less like a jarhead and more like a girly man. In the final chapter in this section, "A Personal History of Lust on Bourbon Street," I construct Bourbon Street in New Orleans as a location that opens possibilities by permitting, under careful control, presentations of sexuality. Here, I write against the idea that Bourbon Street is a site of exploitation as I try to demonstrate how displays of desire and pleasure are taken in, considered, and either adopted or rejected.

Cultural rules for doing appropriate gender and sexual performances have in recent years taken on considerable latitude, but culture still censures with words, with its laws and judicial system, and with physical violence. Leaning in, I write this section with the embedded belief that cultural dictates that harm are dictates to discard. I write toward a better future, a better self.

Chapter 10
Making My Masculine Body Behave

I have been called forth, called to the theatrical and cultural stage, called to move my performing body as an ideological and disciplined subject. This interpolation turns my body into a site that is worked upon and into a source for understanding. I maneuver and am maneuvered among the scripts I encounter, sometimes consenting, sometimes resisting, but never escaping the apparatus of it all. I am caught, tethered to the system of my own and others' making. I am an actor performing life. I have been called forth to offer, using Constantin Stanislavski's vocabulary for actor training, an autoethnographic essay that explores my performances as a man, a man who does and does not measure up to the cultural ideal. I juxtapose cultural scripts against personal experience in order to demonstrate the tensions that emerge as I try to negotiate the masculine roles I have been asked to play.

So I speak now to tell how my masculine body does its part, to show how the regimen of culture and performance has placed me on the social and aesthetic stage. Scripted, my body knows what to perform and when to applaud, and it knows what pushes and pulls against its own desires. My masculine body, trained and content as well as alienated and restless, is ready to share the story of how it has and has not come to behave, of how, in the terms of the Stanislavski method, it has and has not learned to play its part.

Given Circumstances

Written in keeping with type, I am a central character. My body reads: white, middle-class, middle-aged, able-bodied, heterosexual male, a member of United States citizenry. Such a body is familiar, known in most places, unremarkable except in the fact that it moves about simultaneously with and without notice. It holds center stage without thinking, without questioning if it belongs there, without wondering who else might want to speak. It is always there. It calls everything into its light; it seldom looks into the shadows. Such a body dresses in privilege. It speaks its desire in long monologues, unchallenged except for a few minor disruptions. Out of courtesy, it may at times listen to others, but it is never silent for long. A bit of time here or a little space there is a small sacrifice for keeping everything and everyone in place. Except for a slight amount of liberal guilt, it is for those who match the type an easy role to play. The scripts are well-known, performed again and again. Listeners know what to expect and calmly wait to hear what they have heard many times before. There are consequences, no doubt, if one fails to fulfill those expectancies. There can be nothing out of line without an eyebrow beginning to rise, without whispers behind the back, without some self-doubt. But when everything is in order, such performances happen without needing further direction. Sufficient rehearsal is evident. The list of dos and don'ts was distributed at birth. Everyone knows, perhaps too well, the part they are to play.

So I won't tell of my childhood friend, Kerry, who taught me the joys of playing jacks: the flip of the hands to pass ones-ies, the quick run through tens-ies, until the harder "eggs in the basket," "pigs in the pen," and "sheep over the fence." Kerry never complained about the advantage of my larger male hands, perhaps because she always won. And I won't tell how Kerry taught me the usefulness of the flat stone when playing hopscotch or how to anticipate the swing of the jump rope. And I won't tell of the sheer pleasure of skipping down the street, arm in arm, until we heard the call for dinner.

And I won't tell how my large body may look strong but isn't; how fighting, whether on the playground or in Vietnam, is something I never wanted to do; and how the violence of football always kept me from wanting to participate. I've never liked considering my body as a weapon or a target. That's why, when I learned that boxing would be a part of the daily activities, I begged my parents to let me stop going to summer camp. That's why, after I was given a 22 pistol, I never wanted to shoot it. That's why, when I sense I must protect those I love, I wonder if I can.

And I won't tell how my wife found a piece of clothing in my closet that a previous partner had made for me on my request for a robe like the one Jesus wore. I imagined a flowing white garment of cool cotton, sleeves swinging in the wind as I raised my arms. Instead, she made a sleek, polyester, flowery, full-length dress that clung to the bulges of my body as if it had invented static cling. I wore it only the night it was given to me, but there it hung, convincing my wife of my desire to cross-dress. "If that is what you want to do," she said with understanding, "I can accept it." Even after explaining the circumstances of its presence, I wonder if she still thinks on nights when I am alone that I will dig into the bottom of her make-up case for some abandoned blush and will rummage through her lingerie and slip into the silkiest of her silky wear.

The given circumstances are in place, made over and over. This stylized repetition of acts, as Judith Butler (1990) would have it, demands only proper tellings, proper doings. So I keep to myself those behaviors that are off script. I keep them to myself so that I can continue to have a part in the ongoing play. I keep them to myself for my own rewards and at my own expense.

Objectives and Super-Objectives

Julia T. Wood, summarizing James A. Doyle's work, *The Male Experience*, tells me that I have five basic directives or, in Stanislavski's terms, super-objectives: don't be female, be successful, be aggressive, be sexual, and be self-reliant. For the play, as written, to work, never lose sight of the super-objectives, never forget the ultimate goals, never forego the driving force of the action. Make sure each objective is connected to the super-objectives so that a through-line of action is established. And most of all, remember there will be obstacles to overcome, counteractions designed to keep actors from achieving their goals. Actors must be vigilant.

Don't be female. Since others have been cast as female, don't confuse the roles. There are only two parts to be played, one written as inferior to the other. Otherwise, the action is too difficult to read. Make each objective clear, precise. All physical and psychological actions must convey that the actors are on stage to perform properly their gender roles. Some actors find it useful to break down their objectives into units and beats. For example, to help accomplish the super-objective, don't be female, the actors may establish the objective to walk in a masculine manner. This action can be broken down into a smaller unit, such as, to begin walking without swinging the hips, and further, into beats, such as, to remove hands from hips and to extend the chest.

Most critics would say that I achieve this super-objective with a degree of skill. They see a large, lumbering body, dressed in jeans and sports coat. They remember that in my youth I was fairly coordinated and active, even participated on several teams. They hear my deep voice and boisterous laugh. They see the space I take. Less noticeable, however, are those actions that might give the critics some pause. For instance, I prefer, in general, the company of women. I love how they can maneuver conversation, moving from the frivolous to the profound on a single breath, pulling words from my mouth I never knew I had, making talk feel like a hug. Their performance astounds me. I want to do what they do in those moments of exchange, and I will gladly give up any night with men for the pleasures of such connections.

Be successful. The major way to recognize if this super-objective has been reached is to count each actor's money. The actors who have the most money and who have the most power are often considered the most masculine. Displays of wealth, such as wearing designer clothing, driving expensive cars, and living in gated communities, are particularly effective actions for capturing this super-objective. Always compare. Perhaps prestige might substitute for economic gain, but such replacements may put at risk achieving the actors' goals. Audiences may see prestige as too soft, too weak, and ultimately, lacking power and the ability to act.

I lack the conviction to play my role when I remember my uncle Gene who worked at the mill my grandfather owned but refused to join management. Instead, he led the workers out on strike against his own father. When his father died, he refused to accept the mill as his inheritance. He has lived his life escaping the burden of having money. I have always admired his power to choose. But, I also remember listening to my brother and father talk in a language completely unfamiliar to me about their latest project for making money. As they went on and on, I would sit in silence, feeling myself getting smaller and smaller. I saw myself as insignificant, unworthy, inadequate. I was the character, perhaps referenced once or twice, but who never made an entrance.

Be aggressive. Actors who effectively execute this super-objective often do so with easily identifiable physical and psychological actions: Always have the last word, always get the most of everything, always win. Don't let anyone else get ahead, don't ever back down, don't be afraid to use force when needed. Gather allies, form coalitions, create nations. Fight, develop weapons, drop bombs. Claim it is a matter of self-defense. Believe you are always right.

Except for my views on Republicans, I always question if I am right. Such actions put into suspicion my effectiveness in playing the masculine role. While I would be more likely to chew off my toes than support a Republican candidate, I can be indecisive, hesitant, wishy-washy. I seldom take command or order. I would rather not be in charge, would rather not impose. Aggressiveness, to some extent, may have been educated out of me. Even so, I find myself, despite myself, admiring men who have control of every situation, who master whatever they pursue, who come out on top. I often find myself lacking.

Be sexual. Perhaps this is the most difficult super-objective to achieve since its accomplishment often depends upon the actors' abilities to suggest that it is not an objective. Stanislavski's notion of internal and external objectives is particularly helpful here. The internal objective to have sex with a person playing the opposite role, for example, may require that masculine actors enact external behaviors that appear at odds with that desire. In other instances, to indicate regard through compliments, gifts, and entertainments, or to clean oneself as well as one's environment may help actors reach their goal. Failure to meet this super-objective will surely call into question mastery of the role.

I do meet the minimum requirements here. I have two children. But, instead of conquest or consummation, I long for the comfort of a body next to mine, hand resting on leg, head against heart, and the gentle moving of fingers through hair. In other words, I love to snuggle, prefer it, really, most of the time, to the hard, involved work of climax. There is an intimacy there that intercourse just doesn't have. I seek, not rising action, but dénouement.

Be self-reliant. This super-objective insists upon its accomplishment without the help of others. Do not ask for counsel, even in times of crisis. Do not seek out friends when troubles come, even in times of emergency. Do not turn to lovers for comfort, even in times of despair. Stand tall, tough it out. Be a man. And if on some occasion a tear might collect in the corner of your eye, do what you can to hide it. Otherwise, the role will lack credibility.

Perhaps here is where my greatest work still needs to be done in order to fully capture the role. If I need my oil changed, I find a mechanic. If my faucet is leaking, I locate a plumber. If I want shelving, I hire a carpenter. If I can't open a jar, I call my partner. If the air conditioning goes out, if the car beaks down, if the computer gets a virus, I whine. I can be helpless—a sad state for a real man. And I haven't even mentioned those times when I have been pulled to tears, when I have gotten strength from the kindness and generosity of women, when I have allowed myself to write about things no real man should write about.

Assessing my enactment of my masculine role, I know I fall short. I just have too many female qualities, and I'm not successful, aggressive, sexual, or self-reliant enough for audiences to say, "Now, that's a man!" At times I have been booed, had the curtain drawn against my will. And, despite my inadequacy, there have been times when I have been applauded.

Emotional Memory

I carry with me from my family image upon image for being a man, for being masculine. I see my father stopping a fight after a football game by grabbing from behind the arms of a college kid who was ready to swing at a guy who was taunting him. My father held that anger back with his own strength. After he told them both to be on their way, he simply said, "There is no need for that."

In my head, I also have my mother preparing dinner. Each night we would sit around the kitchen table talking about this and that, and she would ask me to peel the potatoes, to slice the tomatoes, or to cut the carrots. There was always a lesson to be learned.

There is my brother under the basketball goal in our backyard, dribbling right, left, and then through his legs for the easy lay-up. He had challenged the kids in the next block to play on our mud court. When they arrived, we were shooting around and after seeing my brother's smooth stroke, they decided they had better be on their way.

And I am there, too stupid to know any better, teasing my teenage sister about the size of her breasts, calling them "boobettes." In a family of teasers, it seemed like harmless fun, but once she was financially able, she decided to get breast implants, a decision she now regrets, having learned how words can make the shape of things.

I carry the women I have dated, lived with, loved, and married who taught me, each in their own way, what it is to be masculine. Charlotte was my first love. We would be on and off again for years. Each time I would write her a poem expressing my love, she would break up with me.

Linda was a blind date. I had never met her before I picked her up at her house. I escorted her to my car and once inside, she asked, "Do you know what I have in my pants?" "No," I answered. "A pussy," she said, unbuckling her pants to show me the pictured kitten on her underwear resting on her pubic hair. We went straight to my apartment. I never called her again.

I fell into Cheryl's arms shortly after my first wife left. She left with Cheryl's husband and my friend. Cheryl nursed me back into health, and then we parted, no longer able to live in debris.

Carolyn dared me to spit beer in her face. Drunk, I accepted the dare. After that, she wouldn't stop calling.

Beth was a theatre major who always played the part of the ingénue. We had been seeing each other for some time. One night, right after we had made love, Beth said, "Don't take this personal, but I don't think we should see each other any more. You really don't turn me on."

Liz and I were arguing about something, it was getting late, and I had a lot to do the next day. "I've got to get some sleep. I'm going to bed," I said, walking away from our unresolved issues. "You can't do that," she called after me. I got undressed and slipped into bed. I was lying on my stomach under the covers trying to put our quarrel out of my mind when she jumped on my back and started punching the back of my head. Raising my arm to block the next blow, I turned, perhaps too quickly, and she fell off the bed, hitting her head against the wall. "I never thought of you as someone who would hit a woman," she screamed. "I didn't hit you," I yelled back, but I was surprised by my own strength. The next day, she moved out.

Claire's two children were finally accepting that I'd be around when I decided I didn't want to be around any longer. Since I was at a time in my career when I was mobile, I got another job in another state. I said I wanted to be closer to my son, which, in part, was true. Claire said she understood. It ended with us saying we would always be close. I haven't spoken with her or her kids since I left.

I carry my friends, those boys and men who were models of what to do and what not to do if I wanted to be a man. Tom, Jake, Bill, and myself, all first year students in college, decided we should pile into my old Impala and drive from Dallas to other side of the U.S./Mexican border where we had heard we would find a house of prostitution called Papa Guyos. The rumors, it turned out, were true. Two blocks beyond the border it was there. Once inside, we did what such places encourage you to do. Bill actually became so enamored with a woman he called Sweet Lips that he gave her his fraternity pin. I confess now what I could not back then: that night I lost my virginity. If it was the first time for any of my friends, no one felt at liberty to say.

George and I had too much to drink and found ourselves on the beach in Biloxi. It seemed reasonable that we would go for a swim. We walked and walked into the water but discovered that the water never got deeper than our knees. Just as we were about to give up, George spotted a mermaid, and it seemed reasonable that we would dive after her, not once, not twice, but hundreds of times. "There she is," I would call out and George would dive after. "I missed her, but there she goes," George would exclaim and I would take a plunge. I'm sorry to report that she eluded our grasp. The next morning George and I nursed the skin on our knees and foreheads that was torn apart by the coarse sand. George and I now live in different cities, but whenever we see each other, we tell that story.

For several years, I played golf with Frank, a middle-aged man like myself whose physical attractiveness had been left behind quite a few holes ago. We were having a pleasant round when I noticed that whenever the cart girl would arrive, Frank would buy a drink, candy, or some crackers. He was filling our cart with all this stuff he was getting but not consuming. "Why are you buying all this, Frank?" I asked. "Have you seen who's driving that cart and what she has on?" "Yes, Frank," I said, "she is a close friend of my daughter." Frank looked embarrassed. "See if you are man enough to get your next shot over the water," I teased.

And I carry all those cultural images, images that say just what a real man should be. I see all those ads: the hairless models, their six-pack muscles rippling, sprawled out on the leather sofa in their boxer shorts, bound by two beautiful women who are offering another beer; the silent man, groomed to perfection, taking it all in before making just the right purchase with his American Express card; and the smiling man, alive again, after taking Viagra. I do not identify with any of these men.

I have all those men who, in film after film, save the day. And I remember that late one night my then seventeen year old daughter came running into the bedroom where my wife and I were asleep. "Someone is on the roof and trying to get into my bedroom," she said with fear hanging on her every word. We sprang awake, and I said, slipping on my robe, "Stay here with your mother." I walked down the hall to my daughter's bedroom, pulled back the blinds, and saw a former boyfriend of my daughter's. "What in the hell are you doing here, Tim?" I demanded. "It's 3:30 at night!" I added, just in case he didn't know. "I just wanted to see Tessa," came the weak reply. "Get out of here, Tim," I said, showing my aggravation. "Roof Boy," as I came to call him, left and I reported all was well. I saved the day but I wonder what I might have done, with my old blue robe flapping open, had it been someone other than a young teenager wanting to rekindle a lost romance.

Memories from family and friends, from women I have known, from the culture I participate in day in and day out, have guided me into my role, led me to act in just the right way and, sometimes, made me question how I've been asked to behave. I have played my part, at times, without reflection, played it well, but, other times, I fumble through as if I were in an early rehearsal. Perhaps I need to turn to Stanislavski's "magic if" to help think through this role I've been given to play.

The Magic If

I start by asking, "What would I do *if* I were a real man?" To be honest, I think more rehearsal is in order. I do want to capture that man who knows, without getting nervous about it, how to fix all those things that break; who moves, without fear, in all situations, always in control, always with grace; who speaks, without effort, making everyone feel at ease, joking, giving, persuading. I do want to have that body, slim and strong, ready for any sport, any challenge. I do want to stand among men and be a man, having measured up by all the sad ways we measure. And I do want others to think that I play my role well.

But if I were really a man, I would begin with a call for a rewrite. I would start by asking if the roles we are given must always originate with that male/female binary that assumes Adam and Eve were given just the right parts to make it all work when we know that many people are not born with just the right parts, just the right chemicals, or just the right situation, but everyone, if allowed, does seem to find a way to make it work. And if I could escape that either/or trap, I would write my body, in all its masculine and feminine sensibilities, unafraid. I would tell the drama of how my body pleases and displeases me as it moves through the world. I would try to remember.

I would try to remember, for example, how I never missed being there for my daughter at every choir concert, theatre production, piano and dance recital; at every softball game, soccer tournament, swim meet, and cheerleading routine; at every parent-teacher conference, award ceremony, and graduation; and at every place I thought my presence might be wanted and, sometimes, even when I knew it wasn't. I would be there, loving her. And I would remember never being there for my son, escaping the obligation whenever I could, sending money and platitudes as if that were the answer, as if that were enough.

I would try to remember, for example, those moments of connection, body next to body, sometimes dressed, sometimes not, but so present, there is a leaning into, perhaps through the eyes, a smile or a laugh. It comes as a surrender, without reflection, without the worry of words, and without pause—the hand that covers two hands shaking because two hands just don't seem like enough, the hug that pulls in as if it wants to stand within another, and the kiss that reminds me that I am only made of flesh. And I would remember the times, out of fear or arrogance, when I was responsible for stopping the connection. I would stiffen, shut down, die. I would be too much myself. I would lean away.

I would try to remember, for example, that to fully embody the person I want to be requires a reaching out and a pulling in. It demands I try in some way to make a difference in this world by keeping not only those I love present, but by staying alive to the world community. It means I have work to do as long as there is social injustice, as long as my privileges come at the expense of others. In such hopes, I find my responsibilities. And I would remember that this man is hardly a man unless I am living with the weight of those responsibilities. Only by embracing what I am called to do can I make my body behave.

Chapter 11
Jarheads, Girly Men, and the Pleasures of *Violence*

In the film *Jarhead,* a group of Marines gang up on another member of their platoon. Held down, the targeted man is threatened with a branding, with burning into his skin the insignia of the Marines. We see his resistance, his fear, before learning this was just a joke. Later on in the film, another Marine who had gained the respect of the unit but is being discharged because of a previous criminal record, is branded, marked in the desire to be what a Marine often is, scarred into manhood.

When Arnold Schwarzenegger calls his political opponents "girly men," he mistakenly believes that the phrase, taken from the "Saturday Night Live" parody of his hyper-masculinity, is just a comic insult, without implications. But he is with each utterance of the phrase saying that people, men and women, who act like women are of questionable value, a step below, not to be taken seriously, dismissible. Schwarzenegger's use of the phrase is a strategy of control, of domination, an ongoing bid for power over others. It is taking pleasure in maintaining the privilege of masculinity. It requires forced submission.

I dwell in the space between jarheads and girly men, between hyper-masculinity and femininity, negotiating violence, its repugnancy and its pleasures. I write to uncover how I have become trapped within a cultural logic that pulls me into a sadistic desire to be or identify with a person in power. Knowing that I have been both a jarhead and a girly man, I write so that I might maneuver without causing harm, without taking pleasure in violence. I write, offering a series of life examples and disclosing perhaps more than I should, to show how being a girly man can be a resistant strategy.

Twenty Tales of Violence and Pleasure

1

When my son was about seven years old, I pulled my childhood collection of Lincoln Logs and cowboys and Indians down from the attic. This was the start of a game that we would play until he reached his teens. Together we would build a town—houses with slanted roofs, a corral for the horses, and a hitching post outside the saloon. We would position the cowboys guarding their town and the Indians in a full frontal attack. After we had carefully hidden the cowboys behind fences and in windows and set the Indians on roof tops and on their bareback horses, the battle would begin. We would gather all the small Lincoln Log pieces, the ones used to secure larger logs, as our ammunition. He would be the cowboys, and I would be the Indians. Taking turns, we would toss the Lincoln Log pieces from behind a designated line in an effort to kill the other player's men. My strategy was to throw hard enough to knock down the dwellings where the cowboys were hiding; his was more of a sharpshooter, carefully picking off the Indians one by one. When the field of battle became too messy, we would pause to gather more ammunition and for the removal of the dead. We would play until one player had no one left standing. Our competition was intense, filled with laughter, and fierce. I hold these father and son moments in my mind with fondness, these moments when I gave my son his first lessons in war.

2

"Be all that you can be," the ad campaign calls and shows the smiling face studying the radar screen, the perfectly toned body scaling the ten-foot wall, and the neatly groomed standing proud. What it doesn't say is that being all you can be also means developing the capacity to kill. Before being sent to Vietnam, I learned how to fire my M-16 on the range by shooting at wooden caricatures of Vietnamese men, women and children. They would pop up from behind small bushes and mounds of dirt while my comrades and I, lying side by side, fired away and our sergeant noted each kill. As long as I didn't think about what I was doing, it was fun seeing how many I could get, winning a prize if I was marksman for the day, feeling the power of the weapon. When I managed to shoot a sufficient number of pop-up Vietnamese in relationship to the ammunition I was given, I was awarded a medal, licensed. I wonder if now the licensing continues with caricatures of current enemy's men, women and children. I wonder whose bodies are sacrificed in times of peace.

3

Driving by cows fenced in along the side of the road, I do not think of their labor, their predetermined fate, or their sacrifice for my consumptive needs. Instead, I say, "How picturesque!"

4

During graduate school, I found myself sitting in a seminar being annoyed by a persistent fly. I thought I might use my notebook to end the annoyance but feared that would prove too much a distraction. With the agility I no longer possess, I caught the fly by sliding my hand across the seminar table. Once in my grasp, I pondered my next step—I could try smashing it to the floor or squishing it between my fingers. The first choice would call too much attention to the moment and the second option seemed too messy. So I decided to pull its wings off so that it could no longer buzz around my head. Slowly, I proceeded with the delicate task. Once done, I sat back satisfied, watching the fly move across the table, unable to lift itself into the air. The instructor for the class stopped his lecture: "Of all people," he said, "I wouldn't expect that of you."

Expectancies both control and perpetuate violence. We are told "don't hit your brother and sister," "turn the other cheek," and "don't be cruel." And we are told "stand up for yourself," "don't let anyone push you around," and "an eye for and eye." Such conflicting messages come from those who raise us, from those who cannot escape our troubling cultural scripts.

Carol Rambo Ronai (1995) writes of her sexually abusive father who taught her at four years of age to sexually abuse her puppy:

> My father and I were engaged in evil; I knew it, I tasted it, I liked it. It was all about power. I was being inducted into the dark side, being led down a path straight to hell, decorated with positive, snugly emotions,

as well as cultivating a taste for sadism. I was getting a look inside my father's mind and finding a way to understand it, to fit in, to be comfortable with what I saw, to be like him. I thought it was funny; the puppy sucking its mother's pee-pee just like my father sucked mine. (p. 405)

"Abuse," Ronai reminds us, "trains some people to abuse: 81 percent of pedophiles were sexually abused as children" (p. 405).

5

Brokeback Mountain shows us two cowboys having a deep loving relationship, and we of a liberal persuasion applaud. It also reminds us that if we choose to have such a relationship, our fate, like theirs, will be either violent death or loneliness. There are many ways to control bodies, to break backs.

6

Besides the spankings my parents believed were for my own good, my first direct encounter with one body wishing to do physical harm to another body was when I was ten years old. A fifth grader from another class decided he needed to fight me to determine who would rule the fifth grade domain of Wilson Elementary. I hadn't realized that one might desire dominion. His challenge came during recess. He stepped in front of the framing of his two friends and said, "After school, I'm going to beat you up." I was perplexed. Here was a boy I didn't even know who wanted to fight me, a boy who had never done anything wrong to me nor I to him. A small crowd of other fifth graders gathered in anticipation of my response.

"Okay," I said, as if I were giving consent to go to Burger King rather than McDonald's. When the bell signaling the day's end rang, he was waiting. We found ourselves in an empty lot circled by young onlookers. He came at me and, in keeping with our fifth-grade pugilistic skills, we soon found ourselves wrestling on the ground. To urge us on, some of the onlookers were calling my name, some his. But as our small bodies struggled, each trying to be on top, I did not feel the thrill of battle, a motivating anger, nor the desire to triumph. Instead, I felt indifferent. So, when he turned me so that my face was almost in a pile of ashes left behind from some previous barbeque and asked, "Do you give? Do you give?" I said, "Yes," but what I really meant was, "Why not?" It all seemed rather silly, even to my ten-year-old self. He left pleased to be king of the fifth grade, and I left pleased that I stopped before having to breathe in ashes.

7

The main highway leading into Baghdad from southern Iraq during the first Gulf War was littered with burnt vehicles and the bodies that were loved by those left behind. Against the barren land, all was grey and black, bombed beyond use. This graveyard, stretching for miles, becomes the symbol of American victory. Flags wave as we forget the cost.

During the second Gulf War, we ponder how to end this illegal conflict. I wonder, as I write the following poem, if a poem can matter:

How to Stop the War

Tell us not of our own heroic dead
who loved baseball and playing the guitar,
who left behind two small children and a loving wife
in a quiet Midwestern town of yellow ribbons.

Show us instead their wounded children
with unblinking eyes, wide as mortar shells,
who lie in some crammed, makeshift hospital
clad in clothing unfit for Goodwill.

Keep the camera on them as they count
the white bandages colored with red,
the burnt faces, the moans, the quiet curses,
the doctors dropping limbs into the trash.

Hold the camera steady, focused on them,
but superimpose the latest U.S. politician
speaking of freedom and the American way
that only liberty, like ours, can bring.

Then, pan to the street where tears race down
the face of an eleven-year-old boy waving his AK-47
on top the rubble he once called home, howling
for his buried family bombed during evening prayers.

And we listen to those who were left behind when their loved ones return in body bags, who know how the stars and strips can cover dreams. So, I write another poem:

The Flag Ceremony

The Marines in dress polish and crease
folded the flag that draped his coffin
to offer an exchange: flesh for honor
and another cross for the row.

Home, I unfolded it, looking
for some sign of him. Each star
empty as his room. Each stripe
a gag cutting into my mouth.

I was watching the 2005 playoff game between the Denver Broncos and the New England Patriots. The Broncos had a four point lead, but the Patriots were on the move. New England's Tom Brady, operating from the Denver five-yard-line, attempted a short pass for the go-ahead touch-down but was picked off by Champ Bailey. Bailey made his way down the sidelines for what looked like a sure touchdown. As he was gliding into the end zone for what would have been the longest interception return in NFL playoff history, Ben Watson, from out of nowhere, flew into Bailey with a crushing blow. The male commentators, my male companions, and I shouted: "Oh, what a hit!" "He was drilled!" "Watson nailed him!"

Recent brain research (Singer et al., 2006) suggests that men find pleasure in others' misfortune; women empathize. How frightening to think that I might be trapped by my wiring, ruled by some prehistoric vestige of biological determinism, controlled beyond reason and without heart.

I have been working on a collection of poems based upon newspaper accounts. I select stories typically found in the back pages, disturbing tales that often chronicle the worst horrors one person can do to another.

I try to enter that world, make sense of it, by speaking from the point of view of those that do harm.

Acid Attack

I guess I was blinded by love
when I hired Ruben to fling
the acid at her. But you have to
understand. She deserved it.
I'm not the first man she tormented,
with her perfect little self, those eyes
round as saucers and so deep blue,
her skin so soft it would swallow your touch,
and her sultry look turning into childlike
innocence with her smile.
You've seen her in the magazines
so you know what I mean.
But she wasn't innocent. No,
not her. She played men
like they were cards, shuffling us
around, dealing when she wanted,
and always holding the trump.
I didn't know that at first.
At first I thought she loved me
like I loved her but then
I started seeing the signs—
saying she had plans, not being home
late at night when I'd call, making excuses.
I'm no fool. I knew what was up.
Of course, she denied it, said
I was crazy and called me her little bear.
I'm sure you've known women like her
who make you think everything
is fine with just a few sweet words.
Well, this little bear came out of hibernation.
I wanted to believe her but, like I said,
I'm no fool. She didn't catch me sleeping.
I had to show her I knew what was going on.
Now, I couldn't hurt her. I loved her too much,
so I found Ruben. A friend of mine who

spent some time in jail for drugs told me
about him. Said he'd do anything for money.
I got my money's worth. That bitch was scarred
and blinded. She won't be modeling anymore.
She won't be tormenting any more men.
I helped us all. She got what she deserved.

I do not like being there, living in that body, trying to find a logic that might explain. But I find myself over and over searching for the saving narratives we tell ourselves. And I wonder what pleasures I take in moving into that violence. Do I, in writing this poem, enact a vicarious vengeance upon those who I believe should get what they deserve? Do I need others' pain?

10

When I was a sophomore in high school, Jack, a senior, asked me if I wanted to be in his sex club. Given my adolescent hormones, I was intrigued. He told me that he had a number of girls who were available for our sexual pleasure. He went on in quite explicit terms about the various activities that these girls would do only for members of the club. But, first, he said, I would have to prove that I was worthy. He said I would have to show him what I had. I complied. He said I would have to show it to him erect so he could measure it. I complied. He said I would have to come so he would know I could do it. I complied. He said he had only one more test. I needed to roll over on my stomach. I complied and when I did, he climbed on top of me, pulled my arms behind me, and let his whole weight press against me. What I remember of this moment is that I could not move. I was trapped, held in place by his superior strength. I was frightened, under his control.

I left this incident with the slow awareness that there was no sex club, at least not one with girls. I also learned that I did not want to have same-sex partners, not because I had some moral objection, not because I wouldn't find the sexual activity satisfying, and not because I couldn't see myself loving a man, but because I fear physical male power. During love-making, I do not want the potential of male violence present. I do not want to feel weaker than the person I am with.

11

Another fight. I was with two of my friends in a small pizza place late on a Sunday night. The restaurant was empty except for us, a young, well-built African-American man who was working the front, and a White man, probably the owner, working the back. In walked four White guys who claimed a table not far from ours. Before long, the White guys started goading the Black man, calling out racial slurs, trying to pick a fight: "Hey, boy. Can't you get a better job than this?" "You sure look pretty in that little apron you have on, boy." "I don't want anyone as Black as you serving my pizza." The African-American man ignored them until one of them said, "Hey nigger, you better talk to me when I'm talking to you." He slowly moved toward their table, his eyes narrowed, focused directly on them. One of the White men, the most vocal of the four, got up and moved forward. They met right along side our table.

"What is the problem, man?" the Black man said, sounding irritated but very much in control.

"You're my problem," the White man answered. They stood for a moment facing each other. Their silent stare could find no way out. The White man threw a punch which was easily ducked and returned with a single counter-punch that landed squarely against the White guy's jaw. His face seemed to explode—blood splashed onto our table, landed on our remaining pizza—and he hit the floor, out cold. His friends gathered him up and backed out of restaurant. The owner came running out, saw the results of the Black man's skills, and told him that he was fired. He took off his apron, threw it to the floor, and walked away without a word. We tried to come to his defense: "It was those other guys that started it. He was just defending himself. He didn't do anything wrong," we argued, but the owner was not persuaded. He would not allow fighting. We paid and left, feeling the injustice and forever seeing what one punch can do.

12

In times of war, male bodies have been the ones given up, the ones sacrificed in the name of religion or state, the ones marked dispensable by those in power. But during the Iraq war those in power became more inclusive. By 2009, 116 women had died (Fischer, 2009).

13

John Fiske and Robert Dawson (1996) in their ethnographic study of male media consumption in a homeless shelter report that homeless men take pleasure in watching violent, R-rated films, particularly when the privileged are the object of the violent acts. They explain: "Certain representations of violence enable subordinate people to articulate symbolically their sense of oppression and hostility to the particular forms of domination that oppress them" (p. 304). Censorship, they argue, should never occur when the subordinated have an opportunity to see violent images directed at the social order (p. 309). What their study makes clear is that one's position has much to do with how one might process violent images.

As a privileged White male, I love media's blood spectacles. I seek out war films that have the hero gunning down the enemy by the hundreds or launching precision rockets on the unexpected. In action films my adrenalin pumps when my champion destroys a hundred cars as he races after the villain or takes on five hired thugs who want to do him in. I slide along in television's detective dramas with the cop who out-wits, out-fights, and out-guns the criminal element. Except for the times I am frightened beyond my control, I take comfort when the horror film's monsters, slashers, or demented meet their end at the hands of the lone survivor. And when natural disasters strike, I am pleased that there will be someone on the screen who will save the day. I cheer on all these fearless warriors, these keepers of the social order, these protectors of my position.

14

He was gay, out, and spoke frequently of his activity as a prostitute. One day, at break time during one of my graduate level performance classes, he said, "I'd like to invite you to my house party in support of George Bush's re-election." He knew such an invitation would not be in keeping with my politics, and he was smiling. Surely, I thought, he is pulling my leg.

"You're not really having house party for George Bush?" I questioned.

"Yes, I am. Next Thursday," he replied, still smiling. Surely, I continued to reason, he was joking. Surely he wouldn't be supporting a man who advocates a constitutional amendment banning his equal rights.

So I replied, "No, I won't be coming, but tell me where you live so I know what house to bomb." Several of the other graduate students who were listening laughed. His smile cracked and the conversation ended. I thought we had shared a comic interactional moment. I thought it one of his best performances—a clear example of stable irony. Two days later I learned he had contacted my chair, my dean, the dean of students affairs, the president of the university, and the FBI. They all suggested that he talk with me before pressing the matter any further.

"Surely you knew I was joking?" I asked, after he sat down in my office.

"I thought that might be the case, but I couldn't put my guests at risk," he said.

"Well, I was joking."

"I'm glad to know that," came his reply.

"I'd appreciate it, then, if you would contact the people you contacted before and tell that you now realize that I was just joking," I said, hoping to put an end to this situation.

"I'm sorry," he said, "but I can't do that."

"Why not?"

"I wouldn't be comfortable doing so," he returned. "Surely you understand."

"But you know I was joking," I said, both exasperated and trying to understand. Perhaps he knew I was joking, perhaps not, but he did know he had me, caught in saying something I should not have said, placed under suspicion by my administration and the federal government, and trapped by his desire. This tale has no clear resolution—it ends with a slow fading away and an increased attention to protecting ourselves.

15

In the eighth grade, I became a member of our school football team, the Eagles, not because I particularly wanted to play but because, as a boy in a small school, that is what you were supposed to do. You were expected, I imagine, to fly like an eagle, spot your prey, and rip it apart with your talons. In my first game, however, I did not exactly soar. I got confused about whether odd or even numbered plays went to the right or to the left. I found myself mostly standing around, watching the action, except for one play. We were punting—I knew because my friend told me after we broke the huddle—and my job as end was to go down field as fast as I could and make a tackle. Heading down field I could see the lone return man waiting for the punt to reach his arms, and I knew I'd arrive at about the same time the ball did. I heard my coach calling, "Hit him, hit him," and for a moment I imagined delivering a blow with such fury that he would fumble and I would scoop the ball up and go in for a touchdown. Instead, I slowed down, grabbed him around waist, and pulled him to the ground, the way my brother and I would, giggling together, when we would wrestle as young boys. In my next game, I broke my little finger and the doctor said my season was over. I was elated. The thought of hurting someone or of being hurt never had much appeal. I'll let others do that for me. I'll let my surrogates stand in, just like the politicians do.

16

"He knocked the shit out of him." Often when I hear this phrase (or its variations), it is said with awe and pleasure. Spoken in such a manner, it expresses the glee one feels in seeing another positioned without control, without the power to keep in check his bodily functions. He is rendered prostrate, incapacitated, lying in his own excrement. He becomes nothing more than waste, wasted. In short, he is a "shit text," a lesson for all to learn.

17

Kirk Fuoss (1999), after chronicling the long, sad history of lynchings in the United States, after demonstrating how these events were staged as theatrical spectacles, and after showing how these crimes were socially excused and socially sanctioned, writes:

> The legacy, if not the practice, of lynching persists.... It persists in the skepticism and fear with which many non-whites approach this country's judicial system. It persists in the endlessly replayed video footage showing a contingent of L.A. police officers brutally beating Rodney King.... It persists in the contemporary hate crimes intended to terrorize not only the immediate victim but also the entire group of which the immediate victim is but an unlucky representative—groups such as blacks, Arabs, gays and lesbians, persons with AIDS, women. (pp. 28–29)

Dwight Conquergood (2002) explains how state sanctioned executions are "rituals of human sacrifice through which the state dramatizes its absolute power and monopoly on violence" (p. 342). The accused, given up for the "ritual of grieving" (p. 365), becomes an effigy where his or her worst part (i.e., the criminal act) becomes the person. In this "lethal theatre," this theatre of death, this morality play that is anything but moral, the state pretends its killings are humane. Conquergood describes these performances of justice:

> Hanging involves an intricate calculus between the length of the rope and the weight of the prisoner. If the drop is too short, the neck is not broken, and the condemned kicks and writhes in the agony of slow strangulation. If the drop is too long, the head is ripped off.... [With the electric chair,] too powerful a charge, the condemned catches on fire.... But even when electrocutions go smoothly they are messy affairs. The eyes bulge, sometimes popping out of their sockets, and the condemned urinate and defecate in the chair.... [In the gas chamber, prisoners] convulsed, thrashed and foamed at the mouth, and bashed their head against the back metal pole. Even lethal injections, the most antiseptic and clinical of all the modes, are sometimes botched. Sometimes the technicians cannot find a good vein; there are documented cases of them searching and pricking both arms, ankle, and finally going to the neck, taking 45 minutes to insert the needle. Sometimes the needle pops out under the pressure of execution, spewing the toxic drugs and spraying the witnesses. Some prisoners heave and violently choke. (p. 361)

What cultural lies, hidden under the name of justice, do I allow myself? What justice is being served, when justice plays itself out differently on differently colored, classed, and sexed bodies? In what theatres of justice do I perform?

18

To mold bodies to fit social norms, to make bodies more useful, and to produce bodies that are more pleasurable for others' consumption, skin is pierced, genitals are castrated, feet are bound, and clitorises are cut. And I, the proud father of a newly born son, said, when the doctor asked if I wanted my son circumcised, "Yes."

19

Bill, my roommate from my first year of college, and I decided we needed a Sonicburger. We pulled in, got our burgers and began to gorge when Bill noticed a large woman eating in the car next to ours. He blurted out, loud enough for her to hear, "Don't eat fat girl." In the stupidity of my youth, I laughed. The woman drove away, her meal unfinished, drove away, angry, hurt, scarred.

20

On a trip to visit my family in Lake Charles, Louisiana, four of us decided to drive to Cameron, the town of 7,000 wiped out by hurricane Rita. My daughter Tessa wanted to go to photograph the destruction for her school paper. My sister Michele was being hospitable, taking her out-of-town guests where they had requested, but having lived through Rita, dreaded seeing more of what she had already seen. Mimi, my wife, and I were cautiously curious, wanting to learn first-hand what the hurricane had done but unsure if we had the capacity to absorb more sorrow. Ten miles before Cameron, we hit a police blockade—only residents and clean-up crews were to be let in. Michele called her husband, a detective in the State's Attorneys Office. He had connections and within fifteen minutes we were permitted to go on. Along the way, we saw a refrigerator, door sprung open, sitting in a ditch; a car, up-side-down, in the middle of a field; a mattress, soaked and torn, resting against a tree; but such images did not prepare us for our entry into Cameron. Once there, we discovered that Cameron was not there. Where houses once stood, only foundations remained. A roof covered a battered tree. A barb-wire fence, running the length of a block, had captured some family's clothes—a red dress, a pair of pants, a small child's tee-shirt, underwear, a single sock. The Gulf's salt water had turned all the foliage into a sorrowful brown. The ground was caked, black, and cracked. The smell, unbearable. Tessa busied herself photographing the devastation while the rest of us stood in the debris, shaking our heads, mostly silent, but occasionally turning to each other to ask, "Can you believe this?"

Standing there, gawking at others' misfortune, I never forgot that just a few months before my eighty-eight-year-old parents had had to evacuate New Orleans. They left, with the help of my brother, before Katrina hit and the levees broke. In the thirteen hours it took to travel from New Orleans to Lake Charles, a trip that typically takes three to four hours, my dad, his Alzheimer's worse when outside his familiar surroundings, kept asking, "Where are we going? Why can't we go any faster?" He did not know he was peeing his pants. The next day, the 17th Street Canal levee gave way a few blocks from their house. As the water entered, the dining room table, the one where they spent their days, rose slowly to the roof. When the water subsided, the table came back to rest, the sugar and creamer bowls returning to their place. But, all was ruined, all was lost.

When Rita threatened, Michele told my parents that they would have to evacuate again. My mother said she wasn't going. Michele insisted and believed she had my mother convinced. When my mother left the living room, Michele thought she was going to pack. Instead, she went into the front yard, fell to the earth, dug her fingers into the ground, and began to cry, "I don't want to go. I don't want to go." After some time, she and my dad did leave, taken from their home away from home for three weeks. When she tells the story of her evacuations now, she says, "We were the lucky ones, you know. We had someplace to go, someone to take care of us. I know I shouldn't complain, but I just want to go home. I want to go back to New Orleans. I'm a displaced person. Just displaced."

I stood there thinking of all those left behind in New Orleans, those with dark faces, forgotten, ignored, discarded, and of all those that died, not just by the storm, but by negligence. And I stood there wondering where the people of Cameron had gone, those who were still alive and those who weren't.

Back home, I settled into the comfort that comes with the violence of forgetting and the pleasure of not me.

Girly Men as a Subversive Strategy

As a jarhead, I have taken pleasure in my power, without reflection, without regard to anyone but myself. I have sat back satisfied and smug, enjoying power's privileges, claiming them as rightfully mine. I have hidden in the face of power, afraid, unwilling to step forward. Power usually knows who is on top, who dares challenge its authority, who remains under its thumb. Power is often smart enough to detect when it can be deployed. I have learned that power maneuvers its way through violence, sometimes buried, sometimes brazen, but never without brutality. As power's ally, violence kills, wounds, scars. It works by turning others into waste. I have lived in violence, literally and vicariously, forgetting its consequences, its ability to harm. I have sacrificed bodies, my own and others. I do not want to do either.

I like myself best when I am a girly man, suspicious of the pleasures of violence, reluctant to participate in muscle displays. I want to be the person who resists violence, keeps it at bay, who finds no pleasure in others' pain. I want to be the person who questions giving his son his first lessons in war, who would not hurt a fly, who sees fighting as a ridiculous way to resolve differences, who laments when faced with others' anguish, who is more concerned with protecting others than himself, who refuses to find pleasure in depictions of others' suffering, who can recognize injustice, who takes no pleasure in violence. I want to let others to enter in, to empathize with those who are subject to power's violent acts. I want to consider alternative perspectives and to take action when needed. As a girly man, I can escape the cultural scripts I have been given, reverse the expectancies of masculinity's dictates. I can rebel against power's violent authority and find my pleasure in an ethic of caring. I can be a better man.

Chapter 12
A Personal History of Lust on Bourbon Street

The French Quarter in New Orleans has always been a part of my consciousness. My dad's business, the Jackson Wholesale Grocery and Tobacco Company, was located on Decatur Street directly across from the now extinct, two-block-long Jax Brewery that nestled against the Mississippi River. In my early years, the French Quarter was a place I held Mother's or Father's hand to protect against the frenetic pace of the loading and unloading of trucks and the honking horns of the passing cars; the people pushing by, hurrying to their destinations, or the slow stroll of tourists, their heads turning in all directions; and the drumming volume of voices getting a job done or claiming, with drink in hand, the street as theirs. It was not long before I dropped my parent's hand and began to learn the streets, delivering groceries, stocking cigarette machines, taking a case of cherries to the strip bar around the corner. It was not long before this place of energy, this place where my dad was held as a willing captive, would come to possess me, to pull me in, like it did him, with its sticky tongue. It was not long before this place taught me about lust.

In the pages that follow I track my personal history of lust on Bourbon Street, from my early years of peeping through doors I was not permitted to enter to my recent experience of taking my then nineteen-year-old daughter to her first night time encounter with this street of sin. I describe how lust on Bourbon Street has operated in my own life by organizing my experiences around four overlapping themes: permission, possibilities, possession, and pleasure. In particular, I examine how Bourbon Street has functioned to situate lust as an act, within limits, of giving permission, of offering alternative possibilities, of claiming possession of desire, and of giving pleasure. While recognizing the potential dangers of exploitation, I end by celebrating this carnal, carnival space. I proceed with the help of a lifetime of ethnographic work, with the willingness to write as an honest witness, and with the desire to rescue lust from the list of deadly sins.

Permission

"I see you looking in there," my dad laughed, putting his hand on the shoulder of my twelve-year-old body and glancing to the open door of the strip bar. Her hips were slowly swaying to the music as her eyes searched Bourbon Street. When she spotted me, her finger curled in front of her bare breasts, calling me to her. The barker closed the door and said, "Come back in a few years, son." My dad laughed again and pulled me on, past the Lucky Hotdog stand and the police officer mounted straight as the law on top of his horse. Twenty-five years later, I teased my twelve-year-old son, "I see you looking in there." It has always been about permission.

Bourbon Street is a place of liberties where one does what one never does. It calls to the libido with its jazz and bare skin. Like wicked fingers, the dimly lit streets of saints—St. Louis, St. Ann, St. Peters, and St. Phillip—lead to a blaze of neon that rubs against the night. Once there, one joins the raucous crowd, moving up and down Bourbon, looking through cracked doors and dirty windows. Closet-size drink stands in every block provide the booze as the dark alleys invite with their muffled music. The barkers promise, "See what you've never seen before. Beyond your wildest imagination. No cover." The same promise holds if one just stays on the street. Exchange after exchange exposes the sexually charged flirtation with the forbidden. For Mardi Gras beads, women consider and often do answer the plea to "show us your tits." Eyes that follow the man dressed as a female impersonator wonder. The men outside the two gay bars at the end of the strip fondle the place that lets them be. Bourbon Street lets it happen. It allows one to smell, hear, and touch, but, most of all, to look. On Bourbon Street, the pedagogy of lust is a pedagogy of vision, and I am an eager voyeur thankful for the happy exhibitionist. Bourbon Street gives permission.

Perhaps it was because wherever I looked it was there—the legs swinging through the tattered curtain, the nude silhouette gyrating against the shaded window, the bare bottom swinging below its mirrored reflection. Perhaps it was the men and women draped on each other as they made their way down the street. Perhaps it was the booze or the smell of it all. Perhaps it was the late hour, the time just before the crowd begins to thin. Perhaps it was the music, pulsing, beating its rhythm, that had the revelers dancing, spilling out through the double doors. Perhaps it was because my date Faye and I joined in, started moving, moving into each other, leg crossing leg, body against body, teasing, working our way into a sweat, seeing only each other. Perhaps that is why, wanting her so, I pulled her to me and kissed her. Perhaps it was just Bourbon Street, that wonderfully wild place that says yes to desire as long as it is held within limits.

Surrounding the permission to enter, to look, and to participate are many judges, some real, some imagined, all watching. Mistakes can be made in this ongoing carnival, this liminal space, betwixt and between the everyday. There are consequences for thinking there are no rules. Permission only goes so far. Breasts are shown, but are not to be touched. Men kissing men and women kissing women are common, but they are safe only in certain bars at the end of the strip. Men and women flirting are everywhere, but the sixty-year-old man should not try to dance with the nineteen-year-old woman. One can do Bourbon Street right or wrong. One had better remember one's age, sexual orientation, and race. One had better, given who one is, be in the right relationships. One had better, given who one is, be in the right circumstances.

Having used my brother's identification card to get my sixteen-year-old body to pass for eighteen, I found myself sitting with my friend Jake at a bar waiting for the show to begin. Jake, too, was sixteen, but I cannot pull forward by what slight of numbers he managed entry. But there we were, waiting, drinking the first of our two drink minimum. It was early by Vieux Carre standards, perhaps 9:00 or 9:30, and the place had only a few customers—an old man sitting at the end of the bar who seemed more interested in the drink in front of him than in anything that might happen on stage; several business men, dressed in suits, gathered around a small table smoking cigars; and a couple, probably tourists, the man twisting the plastic drink stir stick and the woman, her arms folded across her chest, sliding her purse strap up and down her forearm. When the music started, the announcer told us to welcome Tammy and, with unsure applause, we did. Tammy came on stage, stopped directly above Jake and me, and began dancing. She must have seen our wide eyes, our total absorption, and our pure appreciation for she stayed with us her entire set. She took her clothes off for us, shook her breasts for us, and moved her body this way and that for us. She must have been amused to see those two young boys fall in love. After Tammy left the stage, we quickly finished our second drink and left the bar, wanting more than anything to talk about seeing what at sixteen we didn't have permission to see.

Many years later I'm walking down Bourbon Street with my date, Carol, who says, "Let's go to a strip show. I've never seen one."

"You really want to?" I ask, wondering if she is just saying that because she caught me peeking into the strip bars. I've always believed that as a man on a date, I might be forgiven if I steal a glance, but only if such looking carried no hint of desire.

"Yes, it will be fun." So, in we go, a bit unsure about our decision. I select a table a couple of rows back, not wanting to appear too interested. We order drinks from a scantily clad woman who we guess is one of the dancers. Settling in, we begin to watch. I try making a few passing comments without giving any indication that I find the strippers seductive. "Now, that would be hard to do." "She seems to be enjoying her work." "Do you think their pasties ever fall off?" My comments garner little response. Carol seems engrossed and when one of the strippers comes to our table to ask if we liked her dance, Carol reaches in her purse and pulls out a five for her. "Yes, yes. You were wonderful," she says.

The show continues and I find myself watching Carol watch. I wonder if Carol is simply intrigued by what she had never seen before, if she is imagining herself on stage, or if, feeling a slight moisture between her legs, she is surprised by her own awakening desire. After a while, I blurt out, "I think you are really enjoying this." The comment seems to pull Carol away from the stage and push her away from me. She gulps the last of her drink and we leave. We walk Bourbon a while longer, hardly talking, gathering ourselves back into ourselves. A trust has been broken. We are not sure which one of us is judging the other. It is our last date.

Permission carries its boundaries. It pulls you in with its sweet promises and then reads its rules. Sometimes the rules are easily understood, sometimes not, but you know that pushing beyond the permitted is not permitted. There is no letting the dog off the leash, if you want to find your way back home. There is always someone watching, perhaps the steady police, perhaps your nosy neighbor or a colleague, perhaps someone from your church or synagogue, perhaps your partner who you thought you left home. There is always someone to tie another knot. There is always a troubling and tangled tether. It may be loosened, but never undone, for you are always watching out for the watchers. You are always watching yourself.

Permission, then, allows for fantasies to emerge and desires to be acted upon, but permission only goes so far. Some things must stop short of their full articulation. And, perhaps, that is where lust resides, in that tantalizing tug toward the forbidden which restrains as it seduces. To know lust is to know its limits. Lust takes its fullest form when bridled.

Possibilities

Bourbon Street offers options, some that live in your imagination for only a few moments and some that make their way into your being, claiming psychic space and, often, to your surprise, insisting on release. Bourbon Street is a sly teacher. It leads you to what you could be and away from what you don't think you could ever be. It lets you see yourself, wanting, rejecting. It takes you to the "seductive perhaps."

By the time Claire and I decided to enter the House of Leather, we knew they weren't selling wallets. We had been looking in the window display, trying to make sense of it all. Thinking that things might become clearer once inside, I asked, "Do you want to go in?" With a note of adventure, she answered, "Sure. Why not?" After all, we were adults, in our thirties. So, we followed the dark, narrow stairs up to the second floor. Each step seemed to present us with another poster of the satanic. When we reached the second floor, we were welcomed by a muscle-bound man whose tattoos down his arms and across his face seemed to complement his ear, nose, eyebrow, and lip piercings. "I'm Rex. Let me know what I can help you find," his deep voice came. "Oh, we're just looking," I said, as if I were addressing a sales clerk from Macy's. And look we did. There were the racks of clothing, all leather of course, seemingly designed to accentuate the parts of the anatomy usually kept hidden. There were the straps, harnesses, and bindings that seemed to require specialized rigging skill. There were the masks and whips with prices that catered to people of all economic spheres. And, in the back, there was what might best be described as a jungle gym for adults, filled with ropes to use and bars to stretch across. Making sure Rex wouldn't hear, I whispered to Claire, "I want to get one of those." We laughed and then slipped out the door while Rex was demonstrating some apparatus to another couple who had come in.

Back in the security of Bourbon Street, I asked Claire, "Does any of that turn you on?"

"No. Not really. Except," she shyly admitted, "the handcuffs could be fun."

"I think so, too," I confessed. We walked on, thinking about whose hands might be cuffed, until we encountered a distinguished looking man in a tan suit and colorful tie, maybe fifty years old, leading a young woman with a chain attached to her neck collar. She was wearing a low cut black dress that called attention to her large breasts. A small crowd gathered around them. He was giving her commands. "Bark like a dog," and she would bark. "Lick my shoes," and she would lick. "Show your tits," and she pulled her breasts from her dress. "Take this," he ordered, putting his cigarette out on one of her breasts, just above the nipple. She did not flinch. Claire and I did. We turned away and, afraid where handcuffs might lead, decided to call it a night.

Another night would find my nineteen-year-old college boy body in another story of possibility. I was home for Christmas vacation, so I called my old high school friend, Mike, to go have a drink and catch up. We were off to the Quarter and soon found a bar on Bourbon Street where talk is possible. We were tracking where friends had gone and reliving parties we thought we would never forget when two women wedged their way between Mike and me. "Do you guys want to go party?" one of the women asked. Both women were, how might I put this, hot—smiles that gathered you in, hair bouncing against their shoulders, clothes that knew their bodies. A hand was sliding up and down my thigh.

"Sure," I said, still stunned by our good fortune. Even in my nineteen-year-old head filled with sexual fantasies, I had never imagined that Mike and I might be approached by two sexy women who wanted to party. Such things only happened to other guys.

Reading the moment with much greater accuracy than I had, Mike asked, "How much?"

"One-hundred each," one said. "We'll provide the champagne," the other added as she moved her hand to my crotch.

I would like to say that once I realized what was going on, I politely declined. I would like to say that I believed then what I do now: women, although exploited, have a right to work in the sex industry and men, although they perpetuate the exploitation, should be allowed to engage in such practices. I simply elect not to do so myself. I would like to say that I found the whole situation amusing but not seductive. If truth be told, though, nothing happened because neither Mike nor I had one-hundred bucks.

After the women left, the bartender served us two more beers. "You guys were smart to say 'no'," he said. "You were being set up to be mugged." We nodded as if we knew that all along. We left a large tip for the lesson learned.

Another night, another story. The marquee advertises them as female impersonators. The men/women sing, dance, and strip only to the point where you are kept wondering. More often than not, when-ever I take visitors to the French Quarter that is the show they want to see. Perhaps their fascination is because the possibility of changing over seems so removed from their experience. They think, without much reflection, I am what I am. Jackie was no exception as we sat in the third row watching the show.

"Do you call them transvestites or drag queens? Or, what's that oth-er word: transsexuals?" Jackie wanted to know. She was studying them hard, the way an anthropologist might study an exotic ritual.

"I imagine each performer would have his or her own preferred term," I answered.

"They're amazing," Jackie offered. "If you saw any of them walking down the street, you wouldn't be able to tell."

"You know, sometimes they'll use a female to confuse you even more. A Victor/ Victoria kind of thing," I said.

Jackie continued her examination. After a while, she blurted out, "It's their hands and Adam's apple that give them away." She sat back with the satisfaction of someone who had just completed a puzzle. She seemed to relax. Then, she asked, "Do they have male impersonators?"

"Not that I'm aware of, not on the strip."

With a little glint in her eye, she said, "I think I could pull that off."

"Yeah," I replied, "but would anyone pay to see you do it?"

"That's not the point," she shot back.

Possibilities, I've learned, come at a price, both economically and personally. Flirting with maybe can become a yes or a no, but there is always a cost. The barkers seem to call, "For just a few dollars, learn what you can see. Learn what you can live. Learn the new you." The imaginable offers choices, and change calls for adjustments. It is always a question of how much you are willing to pay. For a price, Bourbon Street thematizes and locates lust so that desire can grab hold. In this grocery store of possibilities, there are many brands, each with its own taste and flavor, each with the promise of satisfaction. Variety may be its own spice, but each serving asks what you can digest. Sometimes, you just dig in. Other times, what is placed before you makes the stomach turn.

Possibilities, then, taunt the set, trouble the secure, and tease until assurance weakens. Weak, the flesh is susceptible, open to healing delights and to debilitating disease.

Possession

I have never stopped hearing its call. Possessed by the possibilities of the unseen, I would make my way, usually in the company of friends, to Bourbon Street. I would, guided by my friends' permission-giving comments and laughter, allow myself to let go, to enter another time and place. And in the betwixt and between, I would become bewitched. I would give myself over, soaking up all there was to absorb. Immersed, senses heightened, I would forget and remember myself. I would discover what would hold me. I would learn what images would take possession of me, mold me.

I see myself as a young man going into a sex shop, feeling nervous, but too curious about what might be found there to stop. I slip in, not wanting to be seen. I begin walking down the aisles, trying to appear casual. I am conscious of each step I take. I feel flush as I move up and down rows of videos whose covers picture scenes from within. I pause by some, even lift them off the shelf, and wonder. In the back room are sex toys, some comic. I shake my head and smile when I see the candy breasts, the penis candles, and the edible underwear. But quickly I learn that most of the toys are designed for more than a joke. I stand, stiff as some of the implements hanging from the wall, staring at the instruments, devices, contraptions, machines, and tools that share the shelves. I study the plastic, rubber, and glass body parts that seem to come together in exotic and erotic combinations. And all the parts are ready for aid from the lubricants, jellies, and lotions waiting to be squeezed, squirted, and slid out. I am amazed. I inhale in slow, cautious breaths and exhale what titillates. I would like to do more than look, but I can't give myself permission. So, without making a purchase, I slip out the door into the glaring sunlight. I feel dirty. Yet, I know I'll return. And I have returned, never without guilt and never without fascination.

The words, "Fully Nude Orgies, Staged," on the marquee above the pictures of groups of people wrapped around each other, seemingly in some Dionysian celebration, worked on my imagination long before I had a chance to see what the reality was behind the advertisement. I had imagined body after body consumed by concupiscence, uninhibited, free, wild, moving with unrestrained passion, pleasing one another, in spontaneous abandon, unstoppable, unbridled, until everyone, audience and all, gave over to the moment and until everyone, fully satiated, collapsed into a pile of spent bodies. The reality was three young adults, two women and one man, against a backdrop of mirrors that turned three into twelve, who seemed indifferent with their bump and grind and who were, by law, not allowed to touch. Oh, how the imagination might claim what reality denies. Oh, how the imagination might allow what one would, in this age of HIV/AIDS and relational commitment, never do. Oh, how the imagination might mesmerize. Oh, Bourbon Street! Oh, Bourbon Street, how you bring relief from the forces that hold, how you let me escape from the real.

Along side the images that pull me in are those that trouble and haunt, that push me away, but refuse to leave. I cannot forget the young woman on the balcony, drunk, who, encouraged by the frenzy of chants to "show me your tits," took off her pants and had her partner lift her over his shoulder to show the crowd much more than they had asked to see. The crowd did not cheer as they did when they convinced others to expose their breasts; instead, they seemed stunned, silenced, sad. What had been playful turned lewd, vulgar. To remain a witness felt lecherous, a failure of moral discipline or restraint. The crowd, myself included, moved on. I made my way to the end of Bourbon Street and decided it was time to head home. On my way back, I saw that she was repeating her performance.

Another night I found myself in a cheap strip club with several male friends. We were drinking, having a good time, without paying much attention to the show. Then, she came on stage: a woman, perhaps thirty-five, thick, carrying more pounds than you'd expect on a stripper, blond hair, unwashed, tangled, faded costume which, with little fanfare, she abandoned. She danced, if one could call it that, as if she were trying to keep a hula hoop going. Slightly out of rhythm, her angry hips thrust back and forth and from side to side. But it was her face that I cannot forget. She never smiled, never made eye contact with anyone, never changed expression. She just stared straight ahead, eyes glazed, disconnected from her body and us. It was a face that knew she danced too many nights with a body that was greeted with indifference. It was a face of regret.

"Let's get out of here," one of my friends suggested. On the street, we realized that she had danced away our drunkenness. We did not talk about what we had seen. It was too tragic, too disturbing. We simply departed, carrying her with us. Her dance of despair became our despair. We took her in because she was, at least at that time, not just a stripper. She came with us, stripping us of the pretense. Now, many years later, I know she still lives in me, reminding me of what is at stake when we pursue our lustful pleasures.

Possession carries a burden, a burden to act, even if pursuing your desires is what you might at times consider against your better judgment, and a burden to live with images that won't let you rest. Lust may require maneuvering until you can give yourself permission to do what you want to do, and it may insist on suppressing what you don't want to know. But, when you can surrender to the seductive moment, you are suspended, above and in it all, carried to the carnal and created by the body's promise. Possessed, you are what claims you.

Pleasure

Pleasure comes when there is no hint of regret. I take no pleasure from the woman whose partner burns her breasts with his cigarette, from the young woman on the balcony who exposes herself for a disapproving crowd, or from a stripper who drives her customers away with her anguish. Perhaps I am wrong, but I cannot help but believe that they do or will regret their behaviors. Perhaps I am only exposing in such a claim my own desires, my own sense of what is right. I do not want to participate nor do I want others to participate in activities that bring regret. For me, there is no pleasure in pain. I know that some other moralist, wanting everyone to believe as he or she does, could assert that anyone who even enters into the Bourbon Street den of sin will come to regret their behavior, will come to pain. Yet, when everyone seems to come together in playful interaction, feeling free, fully conscious of the implications of their actions, consenting without coercion, then I welcome the collective celebration. And when everyone seems to flirt with the forbidden, without regret, without going beyond their own limits, then I applaud the alchemy of fleshy seductions. And when everyone seems ready to open themselves to the pleasures that our minds and bodies allow, to their sensuous being, honoring our human nature, our carnival lives, then I want to join in, to be immersed. I want to be a part of the festival.

I can hear the Bourbon Street revelry now: the barkers calling us forward, the competing music insisting upon its own beat, the whispered secrets, the rumble of hundreds of voices rolling down the street, punctuated by sporadic cheers, and the laughter—hearty, cautious, teasing, embarrassed, shared. I can feel the bodies, some soft, some hard, that rub against me as they pass, the warmth of the crowd as it blocks the wind and makes its happy way down the street, and the arms and hands, so generous, so giving, that might take me into their grasp. I can see the cars and cabs trying to push through the human flesh at each corner, the advertisements filled with promises, and the doors that open just long enough to provide a glimpse. I can see myself there, ready to give myself over to the party of sweet pleasures, ready to let the night slide over me, ready to surrender to its smooth, salacious seduction.

That is the place I brought my nineteen-year-old daughter for her first night time visit to Bourbon Street. I brought her under the protection of her father and without hesitation, believing that she was now of an age to be given permission. Of course, she would have preferred to pursue this adventure with her friends rather than her father, but they were not available since we were away from home, in New Orleans, visiting family. So, in good spirit, we started our adventure. After finding a place to park, we made our way to Bourbon and began to stroll. Soon, I spotted a place to get drinks, bought two, a diet coke and a daiquiri, and handed her the daiquiri.

"Is this for me?" she asked.

"If you want it," I answered. She smiled and took the drink. We continued walking, taking it all in.

"Did you know that was a female impersonator you just passed?" gesturing back over my shoulder to the woman who was working the door.

"No it wasn't," she said incredulously.

"Go back and take another look," I encouraged. She walked back, passed once and then again, looking as hard as she might. I leaned against a nearby building and watched her.

"How did you know?" she wanted to know.

"It isn't hard, sweetheart, when you notice the sign above the bar," I said pointing. About a block further on, we found ourselves in front of a window display of a shop selling lingerie and stripper costumes.

"Do you want to go in?"

"Okay," she said tentatively, afraid perhaps that I might not approve.

We giggled our way through the racks of clothes, considering which outfit might be best to buy for her grandmother. Looking for more clothes, we turned together and noticed what we had not noticed before: a wall of sex toys. Her jaw dropped and, after a moment, her eyes followed. Without acknowledging what had just come into view, I asked as casually as I could, "Have you seen enough here?"

"I'm ready," she said, and we were back on the street. We walked the strip several times, and I bought us a couple more drinks—another diet for me and another daiquiri for her. She was taking it all in, making mental notes, and sometimes willing to share what she was thinking.

"You know what I'd like to do before going home?" she asked.

"What's that, darling?"

"I'd like to walk the strip one more time smoking a cigarette."

"Do you have any?" I inquired.

She pulled a pack from her purse. She had never told me before that she was a smoker. I had my suspicion, but I didn't know for sure. I had quit years ago in the hope that she wouldn't get hooked.

"You know those aren't good for you," I said, not being able to resist my parent role.

"I know."

"Okay, we'll walk the strip one more time on one condition. You have to give your father a smoke." We lit up and strolled together, sharing what a father and daughter might in this crescent city of lustful possibilities.

Bourbon Street is still there, living in me, inviting me. I resist reading it as just a patriarchal site of female subordination, degradation and exploitation, a site where sexual domination of, and hostility toward, women is maintained, even though I recognize that there are women who, out of economic need, do with their bodies what they would rather not do. I refuse to see it as a place of sinful lust, even when I encounter those holding an eight-foot cross and handing out pamphlets that claim "Jesus saves." I turn away from the drunk sixteen-year-old leaning against the overflowing trash can, the hustler conning the hapless tourist, and the homeless man shaking his Mardi Gras cup, even as I feel the guilt of social responsibility.

Instead, I claim Bourbon Street as a space beyond the everyday, an enticing place that bewitches and beguiles. It shakes boundaries, jolts sedimentary constructs as it asks for permission. It is there for the taking or leaving. It presents possibilities as it tantalizes. It takes possession as it allows the imagination to play. Its pleasures come when there is for the pleasure seekers and the pleasure givers no sorrow, no despair about the cost, no remorse. Its allure is carnal. It is a place where I have, without regret, taken my daughter.

Part IV
Holding Friends and Lovers

In part 4, I lean into friends and lovers, wanting to tell how those who have entered my life claim, for better or worse, residency. I move about the structures we have built together. Some are sturdy, substantial, a place of comfort; some seem worn, call for attention, require repair; others have disintegrated, broken down into nothing more than a vaguely remembered time. I seek the design of these relational structures, the blueprints of their arrangements. I reach for configurations of connection, leaning in to find what went wrong and what went right. I hold my friends and lovers with love and loss, trying always to remember what is at stake, foundational.

"The Pull and Push of Friendship," chapter 13, uses the push/pull metaphor to define friendships from my life. In the chapter, I celebrate, contemplate, and lament friendships present and past. I search my life history for the relationships where I have and have not been the friend I've wanted to be. It is always a matter of taking in. I see myself and others pulling in and pushing away. Chapter 14, "Evidence of Love," tries to surround love by pointing to what I see as signs of its presence. It works with images, vignettes, and poetic glimpses to call forth what perhaps cannot be satisfactorily named. It offers, then, not a definitive or operational conception of love, but a feel for its presence. In chapter 15, "Relational Development and Deterioration: Some More of the Story," I present a series of poems that attempt to capture the feel of how relational partners come together and fall apart. Using the lyric "I" to tell of the joy and pain of relationship formation and deterioration, I offer poems based upon my own and others' experiences. Some of the poems come straight from my relational history, some arise from witnessing family and friends lead their relational lives, and some are speculative, based in imagined relations between partners. "Holding Mimi," the final chapter in the section, is a love poem for my wife. It is my attempt to let words do more work than they possibly can.

The friends and lovers of my life I hold as cherished, mysterious and weighted stones. I marvel at their various shapes and designs. I am amazed at their complexity, their beauty and ugliness, their appearance and disappearance. I keep them with me, know their happy and sad histories. I try to handle them with care; I do not always succeed. Without them, my life would be deeply diminished. Without them, I would hit rock bottom. Without them, I would have little to hold.

Chapter 13
The Pull and Push of Friendship

I am pulled in, wanting the contact, the connection, the camaraderie. Desiring companionship, I lean in hopeful, and I lean in secure. Those I call friends give me some sense of self. They tell me that I have value, that I matter. I go to them out of need. I feed on their presence. We talk and we talk about our talk, talk about our lives, together and apart. Pulled in, I recognize that friendships, as Rawlins (1992, 2009) suggests, operate with dialectical tensions. I feel the rub between the cultural ideal and the specific articulation in a given friendship, between the need for dependence and the desire for independence, between the affection I hold for friends and the instrumental value I see in them, between the simultaneous longing for acceptance and the desire for honest evaluation, between marked similarity and glaring difference, and so on. I reside in such tensions, sometimes feeling content, sometimes not.

I push away, rejecting the potential and pleasures of friendship. I have been pushed away, been found lacking, unworthy. Friendship comes as a decision, a choice, mutually authorized, proven in interaction. My friends and I have put our friendship to the test—there have been betrayals, neglect, dismissals, cruelty, disappointments, exploitation. Some friendships have survived and others have fallen away.

I write now of how I've been pulled in, drawn to others, sought their presence in my life, and how I've pushed and been pushed away, how lines have been drawn, barriers made. I tell life stories of leaning in and leaning away, stories that attempt to offer an affective assessment of how friendship has unfolded in my life. I speak as a friend, wanting to be honest, wanting to connect. I use pseudonyms when it seems appropriate to do so. I keep what seems necessary and true.

Pulling In

Kippy and I would not have been friends if it weren't for our parents. They were friends and, as children, we were placed together whenever our parents got together. As young boys, we found ways to have fun and find trouble. Once, we stayed up late watching horror films on TV that made us so scared that we had to wake his mom. Once, we fixed ourselves drinks from my parent's vodka, filled the fifth back up with water so that they would never know. Then, we made ourselves sick. Once, when we were playing sandlot football with some neighbor kids, Kippy stopped short to avoid a tackle only to find another boy's teeth broken off in the back his head. Since he was spending the night at my house, he ran bleeding to my mother, who picked the broken pearls from his skull. I watched, amazed; he did not cry. When we were no longer tied to our parents' social pleasures, we drifted apart. We went to different schools, made different friends. Mom, after visiting with Kippy's parents, offered updates. I learned he married. I learned he had a child. I learned he was drafted. I learned he was sent to Vietnam. I learned that was where he died. Hearing these updates, I was pulled back to him, back to the memories that keep lost friends present. I am pulled back to him now.

Pushing Away

There's Mike, Paul and George in New Orleans. There's Tom, Bill, and Fred in Dallas. There's Tony, Jean, and Virginia in Blacksburg. There's Susan, Steve, and Jim in Urbana. There's Ed, Fred, and Steven in Detroit. All, friends of location, left behind, as I moved on. I left with promises I did not keep. I left thinking I would be a better friend.

Pulling In

Gayle works at Mississippi Flyway and Pam at Denny's. Both toil in these Carbondale, Illinois, restaurants as servers, serving my wife, Mimi, and me for years. They move about with a marvelous efficiency and a welcoming charm. We like them, appreciate their warmth and friendliness. We feel we have come to know them, picking up now and then little pieces of information about their lives. Gayle, learning that our daughter was interested in performance, brought her a book on acting. "Here," she said, "this is for you. I remember when that's all I wanted to do." Pam, putting down our Grand Slams, said, "I've been here for twenty-six years now. When I started I'd never have guessed that I'd be here that long." Seldom have we run across them outside their work places, and we have never engaged in more than a moment or two of conversation, but we've come to care about them.

I wonder if Gayle still longs to perform and how Pam feels about laboring in Denny's all these years. I wonder about their lives. I wonder if they are happy. I wonder if I might call them friends.

Pushing Away

If there had been a vote in my high school for the person best fitting the definition of nerd, Gerald would have, without a doubt, won. Gerald was a small, pale skinned boy, with rounded shoulders who always managed to make the best grades in every class he took, except, of course, physical education. The teachers seemed to like him, but he was of little use to the majority of students. In fact, from the students' perspective, he was for the most part invisible. He came firmly into my sight, however, one day when I was confronted with a math test I hadn't studied for. "Gerald," I began, "let me copy off your paper."

He looked at me, calculating. "Sure," he answered, "If you teach me how to play golf."

"Okay. I'll be glad to," I said, thinking that I might be saved from embarrassment on the test.

"Deal," he said, and when the test began, his paper opened to my view.

After class, he asked, "When do you think we can go to the golf course?"

"I'm not sure. We'll figure something out," I told him, putting him off. About a week later, he asked again, and I put him off again. This pattern continued until he no longer asked. I'm sure, however, he hasn't forgotten. Gerald remembered everything.

Pulling In

Ellen was tragedy's busy harbor. It would dock there, unloading death, disease, divorce, and depression. And when tragedy was not anchored, uncertainty would come to port, demanding her attention. My job was to be there, to listen, and to offer what I could. We would spend hours together, living with her troubles and thinking through what might be done. I would sit there keenly aware that life is not fair, that the burdens we carry are not equally distributed. I would count my blessings. I would shake my head when the next thing fell upon her. And when my turn came, when once our roles were reversed, she was there, listening, offering her counsel.

Pushing Away

"Don't tell anyone," Jack said, after confiding in me something that I thought was of little importance. I told him I wouldn't, but thinking his disclosure carried no consequences, I soon forgot my pledge and I mentioned to someone else what Jack had said. Jack discovered what I had done.

"Why did you say what I asked you not to?" Jack wanted to know.

"I didn't think it was any big deal," I said, trying to defend my actions.

"It was to me," Jack replied.

Jack and I remained cordial after this incident, but never again did he confide in me, never again did he seem comfortable in my company.

Pulling In

I know Dan from the golf course. He's an easy-going, gentle man who is a terrific golf partner—he knows the rules, plays at a good pace, is quick to laugh, doesn't take the game too seriously, and so on. I've enjoyed many rounds with Dan. Occasionally, we might talk about university politics, but usually our exchanges are about golf. So I was surprised one morning as I read the paper to see his letter to the editor. It was full of fury, attacking the hypocrisy of U.S. policy on a variety of issues. As I read, I felt as if he was presenting my point of view exactly. I was elated. The next time I saw him on the golf course, I opened with, "Wow, I loved your letter to the editor last week." "Thanks," he replied, "but let's not talk about that.

We're on the golf course." I complied, accepting how a golf course can turn into a sanctuary.

Pushing Away

Virginia, by normative definitions, is a better man than I'll ever be. First, she's significantly stronger, a bit bigger, and speaks with a deeper voice. Second, she marks her territory as hers—no one would dare challenge her right to be where she wanted to be. Third, she knows more about sports than I do and is a much better athlete. In short, I looked up to Virginia as one might an older brother. Once, she invited me to her family boat house in Alabama. Given who Virginia was, I thought I'd be in good hands. On our first day, I disappointed Virginia by my inadequacies as a fisherman. After snagging a trout and reeling it next to the boat, it seems you're supposed to leave it in the water until the fish can be netted. On our second day, Virginia was determined that I would learn to water ski. After several clumsy attempts, I almost made it up but fell hard against the water. I was in pain and asked to be let back in the boat. Virginia insisted I try again, and when Virginia insists, well, you do what Virginia says. I fell again and whined enough that Virginia let me stop. On our third day, I nursed my injury from the second day. It seems when I hit the water I ripped three ribs from my sternum. I could hardly move. I was never invited back to Virginia's boat house. I just wasn't man enough.

Pulling In

When university politics emerge, bodies pull together in an allegiance of mutual gain, in an act of solidarity that makes desire materialize, in a commitment to each other on behalf of a cause. After the cause is won or lost, bodies drift away. Comrades become acquaintances.

Pushing Away

The first time it happened I was hurt and confused. The second time it occurred, I was equally hurt and confused. Two different friends, two friends with whom I shared considerable history and with whom I thought I had a deep and lasting relationship, cut me off. I was disposed of like moldy food. In the first case, my dismissal occurred with others'. Even so,

I had imagined that our friendship was something more, something special. No one could explain what happened. He simply tossed us all away.

In the second case, I was the only target. Like a surgeon with scalpel, he strategically cut me, a seemingly malignant growth, from his presence. No longer did we get together on weekends or share in holidays. No longer did we engage in long chats. No longer did we greet each other with hugs. I do not know if I simply became boring to him, if our differences grew too large for him, if he felt I betrayed him in some way, or if some other force pulled him away. I do not know. I've tried talking with him, and I'd leave those chats feeling some promise, only to find that, once again, I was being excised from his circle.

I mourn these losses as one would the death of a loved one. They're losses where I will never fully know the cause. I take the blame. I do not know why.

Pulling In

I am a member of a writing group. No. I am a participant in a writing group. No. I am a close and loving friend to those in our writing group. We, as a group, did not start that way. We earned it by writing over time, across great distances, to each other from a stance of care, of love, even before care and love were present. We made how we wrote with one another our subject, our way of being until we found trust, found comfort, found a place where we wanted to be. We have not always been as present as we would have liked. We have not always written with the care we should have. We have not always kept our promises. But we have always been there, the five of us, writing words that have wanted to reach, wanted to connect. My writing group is composed of my friends. And even if we might stop writing together, we have earned a place beside each other.

Pushing Away

The first time I spoke with Tom I didn't like him. He arrived in town at 3:00 a.m. with his partner who we had hired in a faculty line. He called, wanting directions to the apartment they had rented. I climbed out of bed, met them at a gas station, and led them to their apartment complex.

Tom did not thank me. Instead, he acted as if I had inconvenienced him. Perhaps, I thought, he was just exhausted from his long drive. But as time went on, I came to see Tom's behavior that night as typical—he believed the world was there to serve him. And I, fool that I was, continued to contribute to his sense of entitlement. He and my wife of that time found each other. They left together, taking my son.

Pulling In

Larry, like me, believed in the value of encounter groups long after they had come under attack. We found ourselves participating in one that Larry organized—he was the group leader, and I was a group member. Our time together in the group was intense and deeply personal and, in keeping with the encounter group model we both endorsed, we met each other with what Rogers (1970) would call "unconditional positive regard." The bond between us that was forged in that group still lives, thirty-one years later.

Pushing Away

When Linda called, I was pleased. She is one of the few people I remember from my high school days. What I recall most is that in her senior year, she became ill and had to miss the last half of the school year. Rumor spread that she might not make it. I graduated and went on my way, never knowing what happened to Linda. When she called, I was glad to learn that she had survived. After we chatted for a bit, she told me why she was calling: "I'm trying to arrange a high school reunion. It's been a long time since we graduated in 1964, and I thought we should have one before we all started dying off." I laughed and told her I would try to make it. But after I hung up, I tried to think of other high school classmates. Few came to me. I decided I would not go. Too many had already died off.

Pulling In

Mike looked so serious. There he was, the Mike who always was the life of the party, who always stayed out later than the rest of us, who always drank more than you'd think possible, who always found himself with a different woman, who always had a joke to tell, who always was quick to laugh, who always could get you do things you knew you shouldn't, who always was first to step up if you were ever in need, who always knew where the hot spots might be, who always … And there I was, standing by his coffin, feeling I could stand there no longer. He looked so serious.

Pushing Away

Sherry, my dear colleague who retired too soon for those of us who loved having you in our presence, I miss you, and I am to blame. You made gestures; I let them slide by. You said, "Just because I'm retiring doesn't mean we can't talk anymore." You said, in all likelihood with a quote from some poet, that friendships last no matter what the circumstances. You said, "I'll have the same email, the same address." I said, "Great," but have done nothing.

Pulling In

Chuck, my Vietnam friend, I still hold you. I see you there, playing cards, drinking a couple of beers, laughing. I see you passing a joint, smiling, ready to burst. I see you, helping me, showing me the ropes. I see you talking with our mentally ill patients, doing our job, modeling what needed to be done. I see you as we said goodbye, deciding our friendship would end, that Vietnam needed to be left behind. I see you now, all these years later, knowing I never left you there.

Pushing Away

"Let's get together sometime," he said.

"Yea. We should do that," came the reply. Neither took another step.

Pulling In

I am gathering, pulling together friends, letting them come to me. I see them as gifts that I cherish. Some I keep fondly in my memory, placed in the scrapbook history of my life. Others I hold now, eager for their presence, thankful that I might call them forward. Most of the time, I trust our connection, our commitment to each other. Most of the time, I trust that I will be the friend I want to be. All of the time, I want them in my life.

Pushing Toward an End

Arriving at the end of the stories I want to share, I am aware that I have not identified those I would I consider my closest friends, that I have not explicitly pulled in those who should be here. I do not know if those I have in mind would put me in the same category. With some who I believe are my closest friends I have never confirmed our allegiance to each other. I just trust that it is there. Sometimes I take our actions as proof; I feel no words are needed. With others, I have made statements that establish a friendship claim. Writing now, however, I feel that naming is too dangerous. Who gets named? Who does not? Who might think I'm being presumptuous? Who might wonder why their name is not listed? Who might feel I've misrepresented us or an incident we both see as significant to our relationship? Who might feel I've written our affection too strongly, too meagerly? I do not want to hurt or push away, nor do I want to be pushed away. My arrogance in believing that any one might care is evident.

Reading my stories of pulling in and pushing away, I see myself as fortunate that I have such stories to tell. I've enjoyed the pleasures of friendship and learned from its disappointments and cruelties. Friendship is, as Tillmann-Healy (2001, 2003) suggests, a method, a way of entering, for better or worse, into another's world. It allows for deep human connection and deep human remorse. It is an ethical positioning. By looking closely at my friendships over the years, I see myself, sometimes pleased with my actions, sometimes not; sometimes being the friend I want to be, sometimes not. I see myself as naked, vulnerable, stumbling along.

William Rawlins (2009) asks, "Under what conditions are people allowed to care for one another?" (p. 135). He is concerned, significantly so, with the social and cultural restraints on friendship. I live under those pressures, but I also live with myself as an individual within a cultural context who does and does not do friendship how I believe it should be done. To those I may have hurt, I apologize. To those who have hurt me, I understand the difficulty of friendship, of being present, of leaning in. To those who I continue to pull in, I thank you for allowing me to be with you.

Chapter 14
Evidence of Love

Watching Others

Sitting together, touching shoulder to shoulder on a park bench, without a need for words.

After stopping at $10.00, the amount they figured they could spend, a man goes into the gas station to pay. As he waits in line, he notices roses for sale for $1.99 each and decides to buy one.

"This is for you," he says, while handing her a pink rose.

"What are you wasting our money for," she replies.

"Spending money to say I love you doesn't seem like a waste to me," he mumbles. She turns her head and stares out the window.

"I have the best husband in the world," she asserted as the class was taking turns introducing themselves.

A curious classmate asked: "Why do you say that?"

"Because he loves Jesus," she replied.

When they were rolling her ninety-one-year-old husband out of the house the night he died, she said, "Goodbye, my love."

She told him that she didn't want to hear about what was wrong with him, that she had had enough, that she just couldn't take it any longer, that nobody liked hearing about others' illnesses. He complied.

"It's a question of choice," she argued. "You can either take what I said and read it in the most negative way or you can read it in a more positive way. We get to decide how we want to make sense of what we say to each other."

"We don't get to make words mean anything we want," he answered.

"We live in a context of love and that love colors, even when we might be less sensitive than we should be, how we can understand our words."

He nodded, trying to agree but her hard words were still there. "So," he added, "we live in a context of love?"

"Yes," she quickly returned.

He wanted her "yes" to fix everything.

He would save something from every trip they made. He wanted the record, the held object as a testifying history.

He said he was a bear who desires other bears. He saw his fingers moving through all that hair, twirling around with his circular rub, pulling to lift the skin just so.

She said she wanted her conversational equal, someone who could keep up, who would know the difference between talk that simply said what one meant and talk that engaged, made one want to linger.

She said she needed someone who was physically attractive, not so attractive that people would look at him instead of her, but attractive enough that people wouldn't wonder why she was with him.

He said he required total commitment, that he never wanted to have any doubts.

She said it would have to be someone of the same sex who knew why she didn't want all that testosterone around.

He said he didn't want anyone who was boring, who didn't share his interests in stamps and Civil War history.

He said he needed a friend, someone who he could do things with and someone who he could talk to when he felt the need, but not somebody who wanted to talk about every little thing, analyzing this and that until he would be ready to scream.

Loving oneself, they knew without saying, was the beginning.

When he was in a coma, she would crawl into his bed to snuggle. There, she could pretend.

Every weekend they would drive the 687 miles that kept them apart. They worked out a rotation—the first week one would drive the entire way; the second week they would meet half way; and the third week the other would drive the whole way.

Their respective academic departments tried to honor their relationship and, to permit ease of travel, both were given a Tuesday-Thursday teaching schedule. Neither department was happy with how frequently they were gone from campus. Neither department, given their arrangement, was likely to vote in favor of promotion and tenure.

As they traveled, their minds were on each other.

The couple who has been married for over twenty years sits together at the party, away from others, talking only to each other. From all appearances they are enjoying the party more than anyone else.

"I'm ready to get out of here."
"Really? I'm having fun."
"What if we stay just a little while longer?"
"Okay. I can handle that."

After two husbands, one divorced, one buried, the eighty-two year old remembers the one she did not marry, how he would grin at her, his head cocked to the side; how he kissed her that night when the bonfire was raging; how he walked down the halls of their high school with her by his side.

Years after the love making had stopped, they made love with words.

For Christmas, she secretly gave him a roll of quarters. Calling from the phone booth, he would ask if it was safe. At parties, they'd find a moment when their bodies could touch in a promise of what of was to come. When they decided they could no longer be apart, they left everything and everyone behind. Being one of the ones left behind, he started a ritual of burning a piece of her clothing each day. It lasted for months.

Watching Self

A hand slides underneath a pillow in search of another hand.

Walking on a chilly fall afternoon, she removed her hand from her pocket, pulled her sleeve down, and took his hand.

Sometimes, after making love, the sillies come, establishing the euphoria of the perfect.

In the small lake by the gazebo, the jumble of the bull frogs' mating calls. In the gazebo by the small lake, they danced to the bull frogs' boo-whop, boo-whop.

"Tell me one reason why you love me."
"Because you want to know why I love you."

From somewhere deep in her sleep, she spoke the word "love" and snuggled closer to him. He chose to believe the utterance was about him.

The caresses that insist on just you; the caresses that insist right now.
The pause before bodies are joined.
The hungry sweat.
The slow roll—gentle waves.
The hand, after, placed on the chest, sinks.

"Sweet," she said, as he came.

She brought home a little book entitled *Do You Know Your Wife?* It had 100 questions and a scoring table. After taking the test, one would be judged on a scale from "Very impressive" to "Weak." He feared, after years of marriage, the risks of being deemed "weak." He started nervously but quickly discovered that the nature of the questions would put him in a safe category. He started flying through the questions as if it would be absurd to think that he wouldn't know the answers. He even elaborated on some answers to demonstrate that his understanding was more subtle than the question's broad strokes. After his score was graded, "Very impressive. In fact, downright amazing," his breath returned to normal.

In their names: Little Bird, Pelican, Mr. and Ms. Happy, Ms. Joy and Ms. Celebration, Magic Button, Mudpie, Romulus.

The simple choice, together, on the sofa, television on, watching, only for together.

He was sleeping on the sofa on a cool fall afternoon, arms folded across his chest. She smiled and covered him with a blanket.

"Do you think," she said, "given who we are and all we will have to face, we would be together if there wasn't love?"

He was at the office and she was home when her email arrived with the subject line "Opportunity." The note read, "I'm in bed taking a nap if you'd like to join me." It made him think of more than sleeping.

"On a scale of one to ten," he asked, "How much do you hate me?"
"I'd say about a two."
"Then, I'd say, we doing pretty well," he answered cheerfully.

"Come sit with me."
"Why?"
"Because I want to be near you."
"Why?"
"Because I do."
"Why?"
"Just because."
"Just because why?"
"Because you're such a smart ass."

For several minutes, he held her in his arms, letting his strength find its way from his body to hers. He took her in, felt they were connected. "I love you," he said.

"Your ear," she answered, "smells like ear."

His arms dropped. He pulled away. "I say, 'I love you,' and you answer 'your ear smells like ear'? You're so romantic," he laughed. He decided in that moment to believe she was not without love for him.

Later that day he playfully teased, "If you want to get all hot and bothered again, you can smell my ear." She joined the fun.

Summary Claims

In how "I love you" might be said: The "I," an assertion, an unshakable stance, a relaxed smile, settled. The "love," elongated and tasted; tempting, almost taboo; tender, yet insistent. The "you," claimed, clutched, cradled; a clarity in how to carry on.

The dishwasher emptied, the back rubbed, the bed made, the lint picked, the clothes folded, the hair fiddled with, the present bought, the shirt straightened, the litter changed, the ointment applied, the plumber called, the foot massaged, the floor swept, the carpet tacked down, the cheek kissed, the plant potted, the bottom patted, the car fixed, the arm hugged, everything paid.

There is evidence in waiting, the waiting

    that smiles into the expected
    that never forgets time
    that fiddles minutes into hours
    that stretches to see
    that refuses to wait
    that collects memories
    that worries itself into despair
    that knows its place
    that accepts the wait
    that wants an answer
    that waits, for a sign, for a simple nod, for a yes that never comes.

Words, like ointment, that ease the wound
Words, like hands, that massage points of tension
Words, like stones, that understand the weight
Words, like eyes, that say what is being seen
Words, like blankets, that work against the cold
Words, like hair, that curl into form
Words, like hail, that pound the surface before melting

By the numbers:

> Not the first, nor the second, or even the hundredth time one says I love you, but the time beyond when one would be willing to count.
>
> The frequency in which the door opened to reveal a smile.
>
> The days, months, and years multiplied by the desire of two.
>
> When the equation can only be completed by letting "x" or "y" stand for always.
>
> The significance level is zero; the bell curve is their norm, their standard deviation, and their shelter.
>
> A single notational system that is the calculus of limits and integration.
>
> When years put in doubt forever.
>
> When one minus one equals what can't be forgotten.

> It's found less in those early expressions of exuberance than in those words that triumph over history.
> It's found less in the resonance of poets than in feeling their inadequacy.
> It's found less in the truth than in the honoring of delusions.

What one would miss:

> The talk that weaves in and out of the trivial and the profound, that stitches care with the carefree, that ties together the treads of one tapestry.
>
> The touch that claims, displayed with pride and legally held, that privately takes in what it knows, that gathers comfort.
>
> The investment that was made (the noticing, the willingness, the giving, the storying), that promise of a return.

It's that small, slow smile that comes from noticing, as one would a work of art. It's the happy linger. It's the beauty of simply knowing.

Chapter 15
Relational Development and Deterioration
Some More of the Story

Relationships come and, sometimes, go. Often following predictable patterns within particular cultural contexts, relationships develop and decline, sometimes bringing people together and sometimes pulling them apart. Mark Knapp and Anita Vangelisti (2005) outline a general model of relational development and deterioration, suggesting that as people come together they often move through the stages of initiating, experimenting, intensifying, integrating, and bonding, and as people break apart they often progress through the steps of differentiating, circumscribing, stagnating, avoiding, and terminating.

Borrowing from Knapp and Vangelisti, I offer a series of poems in keeping with their labeling, a naming that deeply resonates for me. I follow their categories strictly even though they rightly note that relationships can display considerable variety in how they advance and I can point to some relationships, my own and others, which do not proceed step by step in keeping with their interactive stages. I base some of the poems on my own relational experiences across my life span, some on the relationships of friends and family, and some from imagined circumstances. Intentionally, no single relationship is presented across the stages; instead, the poems turn from one relationship to another in order to put an extensive amount of poetic data into the equation. With these poems, then, I strive to tell some more of Knapp and Vanglisti's story by calling upon the lyric utterance to capture a feel for relationships, to write into the heart of why relationships carry such importance to us.

Coming Together: Initiating

Just

He just wanted to be held,
close, flesh to flesh,
pressing into warm,
to be still, named.

He just wanted an opening—
a head to a heart,
a hand to a cheek,
a place of telling, of rest.

He just wanted her to want him
to take him in
so that he might believe
a beginning would have no end.

He just wanted her to fill
the emptiness
our lives, such as they are,
make.

Coming Together: Experimenting

In Search of a Love Poem

It starts as a blind date,
dinner, histories, a goodnight hug.
The embarrassment I try to hide
like a hole in an old shoe,
your words work into a quilt,
a protection against the penetration
of silence.

We search for the comfort
of established patterns,
until, perhaps, together,
we might be rooted,
sturdy as flowerless weeds
in cracked cement.

Finding a Place

We must have been looking
you moving with the Monday wind
and me with wind blown hair
when we danced like bees
and led each other away.
With a few drinks and smiles
we caught ourselves in sticky honey
sweet yellow, stickiest in heat.

We burst open when we met that night
our hands hair bodies
joined, melted together
like ice burning.
We are a closing book
of translated poems
matching foreign to foreign parts.
My hands first moved for you
like skittery pigeons.
Now we fly together
flapping against the wind.

We hold each other in silence
you in the crook of my arm
head on my chest, we breathe
together in a quiet pace.
We wait
each day we are apart, we anticipate
each day together, we wait.

Over dry martinis
on drunken Saturday nights
our wanting words are
broken windows eating air.

Coming Together: Intensifying

What We Found There

was hungry, ready,
a taking in,
mouth, fingers, skin,
pressing,

was ripe, plucked
from a moment
of tongues
taking without stop

was tender, soft,
a drop, perhaps
a tear, dropping
onto an onion's heart

Figures

Together
we are a poem,
perfectly formed,
from measured line
to stanza's end,
a simile pointing
each to each,
possessed with the passion
of lovers
just undressed.

Coming Together: Integrating

Naked

Leaves scraping across the street
for the moment, escape
winter's weight.

Held hands
release, sweat
the end.

Bare trees,
embarrassed, wait
in pointed silence.

Clothes on the floor
swallow the moon, collect
the dead.

Coming Together: Bonding

Fragments of Intimacy

1
The smile that woke me
stretching
from ear to ear
was mine
the morning after
we made love.

2
Shelving books of things left unsaid,
I know all things demand their place,
Classified, alphabetized and closed.
It is a test of sanity.

3
We turn as if leaving
is our claim of understanding.
We cannot escape our lines.
Our past is traced in carbon.

Snow On Snow

Held by the snow in our boreal house
we read. Waiting for the forecast, bound
by our blankets, we share the couch.
The cold freezes our words, deadens
our hibernating brains. We belong
to the world beyond walls. A geranium
leaf falls. We could be baking bread
but we are too bored to move.

We melt with the snow as the sun
returns. Our faces shine outside.
Walking to the empty mailbox, we hold
hands like young lovers, then giggle
in our snowball frenzy. We drop
a cold supper of bread crumbs. Only
a nervous sparrow comes. Tomorrow
we should be able to get out.

As we escape wet clothes, your lines
of a faded summer still shiver
for warmth. Flesh on flesh we are
snow blind, your whiteness with mine.
We glisten in the melt of embrace
then sleep side by side feeling secure.

Coming Apart: Differentiating

Once Upon A Romance

We were lovers
like Cinderella and the Prince
except
you wore hiking boots
had straight hair
and drove a Volvo
and I was broke
never found a glass shoe
and travelled by bus

but somehow
on some normal midnight
you turned into
a housewife
and I
into a drunk.

Coming Apart: Circumscribing

An Explanation

The promise they always foretell
marches on worn carpet
veiled in I do, ringed
around the sprung carnations.

The answer to the question
you didn't ask is
yes, once, when you were gone,
when the day was dry as summer dirt.

The response you were hoping for
starts before the no
and ends with eyes falling
away from the burning leaves.

The connection we almost made
slipped by what might have been,
slid away from the bed you left
over the floor's shivering dust.

Careful

I finger my wedding ring
testing how easily
it slides off.
It slips down, falling
quickly beyond our grasp.
We search,
touching the ground,

knowing
how things tarnish.

We survive, day by day,
by routine, by what
gets left unsaid,
by the silence
of sentries
guarding against talk.

You find it wedged
between two rocks
and slap its dull gold
in my hand, saying,
"You must be more careful."

Coming Apart: Stagnating

Their Life

Even on their honeymoon
it began to wane. Spring
comes before summer falls.

Married in winter's ice
on a dead night,
icicle fingers slid

under their own pillows.
Their bodies, back to back,
refused to melt.

Days bundled into years.
They took cold comfort
in the occasional opening

a hand could court.
They cycled through time,
clothed in caught.

And then, having settled,
they storied themselves
bright as autumn leaves.

Never Said

She slid down the moonbeam
of disappearance
into his sad laughter.
She never danced
he never drank
their desire
to tulip
each other bright.

Of course, time passed.
Their house became stainless,
stealing away their prints.
She was always clean.
He was always careful
to wash away
moments
when their eyes might meet.

They settled,
rooted themselves in routine,
recording their time
in piles of stacked dishes,
full closets,
and empty flower pots.
Their children knew
but never said.

In the Room We Occupy

It is too dark
to see out.
Burnt candles
rest on the mantel.
A tangled tape
hangs from the trash.
The bed remains
unmade.

No smells
come from the kitchen.
Nothing
hangs on the walls.
Only the cat
stirs the air.
The ceiling
absorbs the silence.
The rug collects
the crumbs
of our crumbling lives.
We sit at the table
and carve
our own names.

Coming Apart: Avoiding

The Bedroom

She cringes when I ask
stiffens, readies herself
as if about to be struck
as if I wanted to rip
her wide open.

> *I've stayed*
making my presence large
as tragedy. I've left
feeling angry, small
as the word no.

After the Years

My face is not the same.
It sags with the weight.

My lips, turned down,
tired, set against our life.

My ears do not hear.
My mouth is tomb shut.

My black eyes stare
in fear

that this will last.
I can no longer

see you.
I can only see you.

Their House

Their house was made
of pieces, splintered
lumber scraps, smashed
plastic bottles, bricks
chipped, here and there,
cracked, a tree branch,
downed by the wind, an old
book or two, a sofa
stitching loose, springs
twisted from the weight,
shards of ceramic,
glass, rocks, lifted and
carried, a stove that
cannot heat, a washer
that cannot spin, bent
bottle caps, worn rug,
abandoned, a bucket,
once attached to a
deep well, broken
lawn mower, rusted
metal chair, pillows, stuffing
out, torn clothing, shoes
without soles, piles
of yellowing paper, unread
magazines, a television
without its gray screen,
a lamp without its electric
cord, a hammer's handle
without its head, flower pots

with dried soil, thin
wires, frayed ropes, strung
around this and that
until there was a room,
a roof that leaked, a locked
door, held together by
years of daily struggle,
by their quiet anger
making its hateful glue.

Coming Apart: Terminating

Stone, Shell, Feather

On the beach,
a stone,
brick red,
the size of my palm,
smooth as the skin
I cannot touch.
It anchors my hand.
Its weight—
a dead heart.
I carry it home.

A shell,
once perfect,
now chipped, cracked,
spotted with the color
of the stone, empty.
On its underside,
barely visible,
a mark of connection
to its other half.
I carry it.

A feather,
wet, lost to the gull
that flies

against the red sky,
against the wind,
shudders,
then banks away.
It lands, settling
on one thin leg
above its nest,
thinking, over
and over, of one
feather more.

What Gets Left Behind

A chipped coffee cup,
sipped
through too many conversations.

A shoebox of photographs
from years ago.

Pliers, wrenches, screwdrivers,
tools
that hands shared.

Old spices
gone flat.

Green, floral sheets,
faded,
edges frayed.

Poems
you once believed.

A child.

Apart

we are a broken rhyme,
a metonymy
as desperate as
a dangling modifier,
a grammar no one speaks,
adjectives in search
of a noun,
adverbs seeking
their to be.

Reconsidering the Moon

The moon knows the black cloud
and what it keeps. The empty nest
remembers its construction, each twig
a new design. The red lights
turn the corner. There is no bread
in the house that sits still as ash.

History is not an and then;
it's a winnowing, chaff discarded
for the sake of grain, a word
not said, an action not done,
a forgiveness not given.
History is the always never.

The uncarried already arrives
too late. The should haves haunt
the ghosts. The furnace groans
against the cold air. Dishes
need to be done and that moon
is forever finding its dark place.

Chapter 16
Holding Mimi

I am holding Mimi, tight, holding her until we take each other in, sense the connection, until our breath finds the same rhythm. I am holding her, wanting to be there, in her arms, welcomed, close as the two center pages of a book. Our fingers, linked, write us, tell what needs to be said. We turn into the composition of the other's making.

I am holding Mimi, inside—quietly, softly, calmly—knowing the comfort of years, the confidence of "of course." I am breathing with her, breathing in, breathing out. I am sitting with her, holding hands, without worry, just there, together, having earned the ease of silence.

I am holding Mimi, refusing to let go, even when troubles come, refusing to let blame, however seductive, have an anchor. I am holding on, needing her, like a socket for an eye, looking toward tomorrow and the days after.

I am holding Mimi, hungry, wanting her, wanting the rawness of body to body, flesh to flesh. I am ravenous, taking her in, greedy, surrendering to the sensuous. I am enraptured, desiring her, living in the ecstasy of the miraculous moment, born into being, transformed by touch.

I am holding Mimi, with no regrets, except my mistakes, relieved she remains here, by my side, forgiving. I am holding her, thankful, a supplicant at the altar of our connection, caught in desire, always wanting her benevolent blessing.

I am holding Mimi, bound by the beauty of our daughter, revisiting her visits, living her luscious life, dreaming her dreams. We watch, together, nourished by her strength, priding ourselves for the small part we play.

I am holding Mimi, blind to reason, abandoning all attempts to explain, just there, letting affect take effect. I am the judge with no verdict, the preacher with no scripture, the teacher with no lesson. I am crying, crazily happy, just desperately there.

I am holding Mimi, laughing and laughing again, pushing past puns, jumping on jokes, and sliding into silly. Holding on, we are rollicking, rolling on the floor, funny for our own fun, a comedy of our own creation.

I am holding Mimi, inquisitive, insisting she tell more, burst beyond what might contain, burst into disclosure. I am holding her, wanting to hear it all, from the inconsequential pin dropped on the floor to the thunder's dangerous clap. I am listening, ready, taking in.

I am holding Mimi, mindful, managing wounds and mapping scars, moving forward without forgetting how damage can be done, hoping the cut can turn into the scratch, the blow into a fading bruise.

I am holding Mimi, inflated, proud, strutting around town with her on my arm. I, a swollen melon, smiling from ear to ear, marvel.

I am holding Mimi, jazzed, riding the rhythms of our everyday melodies, sliding away from dissonant chords into the harmonious sounds of sweet surrender. As the saints march to our step, I am holding her, juiced up, hearing the music we can play, feeling the vibrations of together.

I am holding Mimi, licensed, coupled by the state, but living under our own authority, having the sanction of our choosing and the approval of our hearts, endorsed by the happy consent that comes from knowing how two bodies might meet.

I am holding Mimi, motivated, wanting to do it right—all the questions duly answered, all the fears swept away, all the fingers properly intertwined. I am holding her, invested, having placed my entire bet on forever.

I am holding Mimi, saturated in history, some happy, some not, remembering how we've kept those times of joy, radiating in them, raving about them, and returning to them, and how we've managed when infested with noisy memories, eradicating them, swatting away those that might harm.

I am holding Mimi, immersed in the immediate moment, intoxicated by my good fortune, unable to recognize a beginning or ending, only a now, murmuring nothing but love, nothing but love, love, love.

I am holding Mimi, trembling, worried there could be a time when she'd say no, no more, no more of you; when she'd say, tying my hands behind my back, no, no more, no more touching; when she'd say, walking out the door, yes, yes free, yes free from you, and I'd be left quivering, alone, holding the air where she once stood. I am holding her, shaking away the nightmare, trusting other stories I prefer to tell.

I am holding Mimi, taking, taking what I need—a touch that accepts, a look that approves, a word that specifies—grabbing, clutching what I hardly deserve. I am a man holding her, needing more than I give.

I am holding Mimi, facing her, filled with eyes, falling into smiles. I, an old pelican, am holding her, flying.

I am holding Mimi, tracing feelings, figuring reasons, adding it all up, calculating rewards as the costs fade away. I am holding her, well ahead, satisfied as a full house, content as a balanced equation.

I am holding Mimi, repeating myself, saying, again and again, what needs to be said right; striving, again and again, to nail it down; wanting her, over and over, to believe that I am here, completely, reaching for her hand.

I am holding Mimi, leaning in, learning to listen, hearing what I can, trying to keep my ears open, available, ready to echo what needs a second sounding, ready to keep what needs more mulling, ready to give what needs to be given.

I am holding Mimi, inept, clumsily making words, babbling on and on, trying to prove a case: I am holding Mimi.

Part V
Carrying Family

I carry my family of origin with joy. I say this not wanting to romanticize us or to deny our failures, but with a keen sense of my good fortune. I was born into a family that wanted me, that understood what it means to love, that raised me with many of the values I continue to hold. We have had good times and stressful times. Through it all, our "relational culture" (Baxter, 1987; Wood, 2000) has remained a strong, solidifying force, an ongoing comfort, and a welcoming retreat. My family of origin has been the blueprint of my making (Satir, 1988). It formed me, made me into the participant I am within my current family. In this final section, I write both my family of origin and my current family. I proceed with love and I hope with sufficient care that they feel that love in my words. Even when I discuss our frailties, our failures, and our misfortunes, I carry them as a locating, lasting, and luxurious load.

I start with "Family Lessons." In this chapter, I name members of my family of origin and my current immediate family. With each naming, I offer a story that teaches, that functions for me as life pedagogy. I take these lessons as generous gifts, offered to me through family history and example. In chapter 18, "Stories We Do and Do Not Tell," I turn, in concert with H. L. Goodall's (2006) *A Need to Know*, a family secret into a public telling. This tale concerns my sister's need to know her biological parentage. My desire is to tell this tale without doing any harm. I have my sister's permission. I believe it is a safe tale to tell. In chapter 19, "Remains," I reach for my parents as they experience the ruin of their home in the wake of the Katrina flood in New Orleans. Relocated in Lake Charles, Louisiana, they reclaim home in what remains, in what they can carry. I try to shoulder some of the load. Chapter 20, "Loss," offers a fragmentary account of my efforts to deal with my father's death. I do and do not find comfort in the telling. At times, I would rather live in denial or would rather the essay never end. I would rather keep him alive by writing and writing and writing still more.

Such tellings are a construction, a glimpse into a relational culture that has much more history than can be shared in these few chapters. I offer sketches, portraits, watercolors, and shadings—all are frozen impressions. I divulge what most often remains within the family circle. I author partial renderings of our life together, told from my point of view. If my writing leads readers to a negative perception of any member of my family, they should leave this book knowing I do not share their perspective. Blame the writing, condemn the writer, but not those about whom I have written. They would have their own way of telling, and I would love to listen, to lean in.

Chapter 17
Family Lessons

We know them best, those we call our family members, by the stories we carry. We share family tales around dining room tables, in kitchen nooks while stirring a pot or making a salad, and on sofas in whispered tones. They come on holidays, in times of birth, trouble, and loss, and on afternoons and evenings of reminiscence. They tell of connections, some strong, some weak, linking generations. Some of the tales we have heard again and again—they have become family lore. They often develop signature status, stories that are evoked whenever a particular person is mentioned and that stand in for who that person is. Others are family stories of our own making, based upon what lingers from our interactions with them, from what we've heard about them, and from being with them, watching. Such tales feel personal, unique, a link between just the two of you. For better or worse, we hold all these family tales. They become possessions, keepsakes, reminders. They constitute, as Goodall (2006) would suggest, our "narrative inheritance" (p. 23). But most of all, they turn into lessons, a pedagogy for living.

In these next few pages, I tell stories, ones that I have heard and ones that I have told or create now, of my immediate family in the desire to make concrete the lessons I keep learning and continue teaching to my children. Some of these stories, known by everyone in my family, are told with great pleasure, feel celebratory; others seem weighted, cautionary. Some make their instructive message explicit, others implicit; and still others emerge as family puzzles, stories waiting for collective sense-making. Some enjoy consensus, feel stable; some meet resistance, mark differences, tell of tensions between members. All, as told here, are my versions of our family stories, spun by me, but borrowed from those I love the most. I share without wanting to do harm, without malice. I tell these tales with love, with the belief that our stories, like the narratives of all families, have much to teach.

Eugene Schaeffer, My Mother's Father (FaFa)

"Your grandfather always wanted you kids to grow up independent," my mother would begin. "When you were just little things, we'd take you to a ballgame. FaFa would spot a concession stand, and then, he'd give you some money and tell you to go, all by yourself, to get something. You'd look up at him as if he didn't know what he was saying, but he'd insist and send you on your way. He'd always keep his eye on you, but he wanted you to know you could do things on your own."

I do not remember being sent on such an adventure, and I do not know the extent to which his intent had a claim. His instruction in independence, or some might argue stubborn foolhardiness, comes to me most strongly, though, in another tale. He ran a mill, made cabinets and furnishings to specifications. He was a fine craftsman, but one day, while he was working the circular saw, the blade flew off its wheel. It spun through the air until it found the top of his head, scalping him half way back. He lifted the flap of skin forward, setting it in place, took off his shirt and tied it around his forehead so that the blood would not run into eyes. He then drove himself, despite offers from others, to the hospital.

Valerie Clemens Schaeffer, My Mother's Mother (Bobbi)

Every morning she would do it. She'd lift her robe, expose the fatty tissue of her upper thigh, and give herself her insulin shot. I can still see the needle penetrating her skin. I can still see the surrounding bruises from the shots that came before. I can still smell the alcohol on the cotton ball wipes. I would sit at her kitchen table, watching, aware of the differences in an adult's and child's world as I ate what Bobbi called "men- in-a-boat," a poached egg placed on toast and cut up so that the little men could float around on my plate.

When Bobbi died, my Mother asked if I wanted a memento from her things. I asked for the glass candy dish, the one she kept filled with candy that she could not eat, the one from which I was told I could pick a treat each time I would visit.

Michael Pelias, My Father's Father (Papouli)

I could tell the tale of how he came to the United States as a young boy on a Greek freighter, saw New Orleans, and decided to stay. I could share the story about how he sold Greek candies on the street before he had enough money to open a little Greek restaurant. I could report that he struggled, like so many others, during the Great Depression, and that at the start of World War II he began the Jackson Wholesale Grocery with six cases of rationed sugar. Each carries a lesson to learn. But the tale of Papouli, my grandfather who at times didn't know where he might find his next meal, most clearly etched in my mind revolves around Tuesday night dinners at his house when I was a small boy. I would always be placed to his right, and he would always decide what I should eat. If I was taking too long or had left some unfamiliar Greek serving on my plate, he would bop the back of head. "Eat that," he would say, looking at the food that remained. I would get it down, already dreading the next Tuesday night's dinner and already beginning a lifetime of eating everything on my plate.

Natalie Pelias, My Father's Mother (YaYa)

I remember her as severe, hair always pulled back into bun, hardly ever looking in my direction. I do not believe I ever gave her a kiss or a hug. I do not think we ever touched. Her English was limited, and my Greek consisted of a few curse words, words inappropriate to share with a grand-mother. She would sit in her rocker, talking with those who shared her language. When YaYa died, the family found among her things a collection of poems, all written in Greek. My Uncle Harry decided, since I was a college professor, that I should be the one to have YaYa's poems translated into English. While Uncle Harry's logic never seemed persuasive to me, I took on the task and, as luck would have it, a student appeared in my class who was fluent in Greek. I asked him if he would be willing for a fee to offer a rough translation of YaYa's poems. He agreed, and a week later he returned. "Do you want me to translate all of these?" he asked.

"I was thinking so. Why?"

"Well, to be truthful, they are all pretty much the same. Each is written on some special occasion—a birthday, a wedding," he reported. "They're highly sentimental and they're heavily rhymed."

"Like Hallmark cards?" I asked.

"Yeah, just not as good," he said sheepishly.

After reading me several examples, we agreed that he had done enough. I paid him for his efforts, and he left the poems on my desk. Flipping through, I saw two translated poems that were titled with my name, one on the day of my birth and one on the occasion of my graduation from high school.

Gus M. Pelias, My Father (Dad)

When I was a teenager, Dad would remind me: "Times were hard when I was growing up. YaYa would take all those little pieces of soap that are left behind when you think you've used all you can and melt them together to make a new bar of soap. There's a Greek work for those little pieces." He would say the word but I no longer can call it forward. Then he'd continue: "Yeah, times were hard. YaYa would wait until Papouli would fall asleep and then swipe the change from his pocket so that she could send us to school with money when we needed it. 'God damn it, woman,' Papouli would say when he discovered the missing change, 'Are you robbing me again?' When I started working at the Jackson warehouse for Papouli, he paid me twenty-five dollars a week. That had to cover all expenses—rent, food, everything. Your Mother and I managed though. Sometimes we'd even give ourselves a night out: five cents each for us to get downtown by streetcar, fifteen cents each to get in the movie, and five cents each to get back home. A fifty cents night on the town. I tell you, times were hard. Do you remember that, Merle?" Dad would end, asking my mother to confirm his facts.

"I sure do," Mom answered. "And remember how Papouli would come over to our house and look in our refrigerator to make sure we weren't spending too much money on food?"

"Why you need all that butter?" Dad, mimicking Papouli, replied.

"Give Ronnie his money. He's going to be late for his date," Mom encouraged, remembering what started the conversation.

"Twenty dollars for one date?" Dad said, shaking his head and handing me the money.

Merle Schaeffer Pelias, My Mother (Mom)

Always a meat, starch, and vegetable—the standard meal made ready for when Dad would come home. Perhaps, a pineapple salad, with a touch of shredded cheese on top and, for those who wanted it, a dab of mayonnaise. There was no eating until Dad arrived. "If he can make the money for this meal," Mom would say, "the least you can do is wait until he's here to eat it." The time of preparation and waiting was always the best— Mom would ask me to peel the potatoes or to chop an onion. I would busy my hands, but most of all, I would listen. It was then the lessons were given. Small talk turned into little morality plays, into life instructions that keep a boy his mother's son. Even now, Mom in her ninety-second year, a meat, a starch, and a vegetable. Even now, although I am less often there cutting or chopping, lessons: "Believe me, Honey, you don't want to live so long that all your friends and relatives are gone. You don't want to be the one left behind after years and years of marriage. It's just too lonely."

Gus M. Pelias, Jr., My Brother

We have always been close. Seldom, though, have we expressed our affection for one another. One day, I found myself writing a poem about our relationship:

The Point of the Shovel

My brother resides at the site
between the knuckles of my ring finger:
a failure of coordination
of shoveling and pulling dirt
that made my half-moon reminder
of the construction of tunnels,
of bridges, and of our private passages.

With each thrust of the shovel
he unearthed our future,

excavated intricate connections.
When our rhythm broke,
he wrapped his hand around
my finger to hold the bleeding.
We are still standing. There.
Blood cementing finger to hand.

Now he is an architect,
a planner of foundations,
boss of bulldozers and cranes,
designer of abutments,
who leaves his mark
measure by measure.
His first project
was my pure white scar.
The point of the shovel
came to the bone.

After the poem was published, I gave him a copy. It brought us closer.

Debbie Krantz Pelias, My Sister-in-Law

Debbie is an accomplished artist. When she told Mimi and me that we would be welcome to one of her paintings, we were thrilled. She led us to a stack of paintings leaning against a wall and told us to decide which one we wanted. We moved through Debbie's impressive collection, both stopping on the same one. We knew the painting we hoped to have hanging on our wall.

It has been hanging on our living room wall for many years now. It is large, three foot by five foot oil on canvas. In its center is a large spiked wheel, its top and bottom eighths suggesting completion beyond the frame. Outside the wheel is painted black with touches of green and yellow. The same colors are repeated in an eight inch by twelve inch rectangle at the wheel's hub. The wheel itself appears in brown, tan, rust, and green, with several rust colored blotches that cover parts of the spokes. Upon close examination, random squiggles cutting across the straight lines of the spokes emerge. They seem like a foreign lettering but don't quite seem to achieve it. They fade away at a distance.

For me, the painting is a study in form. It insists that I see the presence of form while it simultaneously calls attention to its disappearance. The wheel invites completion as it is not fully pictured. The rust blotches cover parts of the wheel and can be read as decay, a slow eating away of the circle. The random squiggles only appear when I am within a few feet of the painting and pull me closer and closer as I try, without success, to decipher their linguistic meaning. The outer and inner colors serve as a framing universe but fall away to the wheel's power, and only after some lingering within the wheel's web, do they return again. The inner rectangle calls me forward, becomes a seductive passageway. What is given is never complete; what is missing is always insisting upon its presence. I love sitting in the presence of this painting, love having it on our wall, love looking.

But getting it to our wall was no easy task. Because Mimi and I had flown to New Orleans, carrying it back to Carbondale, Illinois, with us was not possible. Debbie insisted that she would mail it, and despite expressing our concern about the labor and cost involved, Debbie sent the painting the week we arrived back home. It came wrapped in cardboard pieces, held together with tape and twine. It was clear that considerable effort allowed the painting to arrive safely. Part after part of protective covering was secured. Various cardboard boxes of various colors had been broken down before being reassembled carefully over the painting. Tape of various kinds and colors zigzagged this way and that, held the uneven seams. The twine, pulled tight, wound around in a clear grid. Our names and address were written in large black lettering, center. As Mimi and I slowly removed the packaging, I understood that this, too, was a study in form.

Michele Pelias Bailey, My Sister

Ann has always been Michele's best friend. As the story goes, when they were both three years old, one said to the other, "Do you pick your nose?" The other replied, "Yes," to which the first one said, "Me, too." They have been lasting friends since, best friends although they did not attend the same schools or colleges, best friends although they have not lived in the same city for many years, best friends although they both carry the obligations and demands of family and work. They made their friendship last. And when Ann asked my sister what she wanted for her fifty-sixth birthday, Michele said she wanted Ann to drive to Lake Charles from New Orleans to be with her. Ann drove.

That's what friends do, I thought, as Michele told me about Ann coming to visit.

I imagined them together, my sister and Ann talking on and on, sharing tales in tones of amusement and amazement, entertaining and advising one another, enjoying being together. They have forged themselves over time into a "we." And I wondered whom from my high school or college days would I drive 200 miles to see.

Scott Bailey, My Brother-in-Law

As we often do on family vacations, Scott and I were playing golf together. He was having a particularly strong round—two under through twelve holes. Every shot he was hitting was dead straight and every putt was either dead center or burning the edge. Then the call came—his son from a previous marriage had found trouble again. After he determined that there was nothing at this point that could be done, we finished the round. Scott's game, however, was gone. He started pulling and pushing his drives and irons and his putts were wide, short, or long.

Driving back to the hotel, Scott said, "I can't believe how that telephone call messed up my game."

"What else would you expect?" I asked. "If it had been my son—and as you know, it could have been given the troubles I've had with Doug—I'm sure the same thing would have happened to me."

"They keep us hooked, don't they?" Scott said.

"Yeah, like a snap hook, straight into their trouble."

Mimi Hinchcliff-Pelias, My Wife

Although Mimi has, she'd rather not go alone when she needs to have blood taken. She would prefer I go to the lab with her. I hold her hand and make distracting conversation while the technician inserts the needle. After we are home, I assure her that it's fine if she wants to remove the band-aid. The bleeding, I tell her, I'm sure has stopped. This same person has no qualms about going alone for extended periods to teach in foreign countries, no hesitations about traveling solo anywhere in the world, no second thoughts about taking a taxi driven by an Arab man who does not share any of the languages she speaks across the Sahara in the dead of night. She trusts, in such circumstances, that she'll be fine.

I admire Mimi's willingness to embrace adventure, her strong independence, and I am glad that at times I am still of some use.

Douglas Weaver Pelias, My Son

It's been over two years now since I've heard a word. Usually I'd hear from him about every six months: "Hey, Dad, I'm a little short. I'm hoping you can spot me a few hundred." But since the time I refused to bail him out of jail, I have not heard a word. I've tried contacting him, but all the ways I once knew would reach him no longer work. Perhaps he is in jail, serving time for driving while suspended, but that seems unlikely. Perhaps he found a way to take care of himself and no longer wants my help. After all, he's almost forty years old now, but that, too, seems unlikely. Perhaps he has written me off, like he did with his mother after she refused to give him any more money: "She's dead to me. I don't have a mother." Perhaps he overdosed and, since he was indigent, living on the streets, the authorities could not track down his mother or me. No, that can't be the case. Perhaps, one day, out of the blue, he'll call: "Hey, Dad. It's been a while." And if that happens, I will wonder if it is better to be hooked by possibilities or by realities.

Tessa Pelias Parkhurst, My Daughter

I find myself always writing about Tessa. When she was still living with Mimi and me, I'd share with her what I had written about her. "That's nice, Daddy," she'd often say, but seemed only mildly interested in what I had struggled to put on the page. When my last book came out, she was in college, and I gave her a copy. She was a frequent subject, and I thought she would be interested. She seemed appreciative, but when I asked her six months later if she had a chance to read the book, she said she had not. "I don't know what happened to it, Daddy. Give me another one so I can read it." I gave her another copy, but shortly afterwards I found the first copy I gave her shoved onto a book shelf among her childhood books. She never took the book with her, never felt the need to read it. She has not given me any indication that she read the second copy I gave her. The book, filled with writing about her, has not lured her in.

I find myself surprised that she wouldn't be more curious. Perhaps, too, I am a bit disappointed that she has such little interest. I wonder if she is so confident in my love for her that she feels little need to read about it. I wonder if my loving words embarrass her. I wonder if the fact that she is in her mid-twenties accounts for her response. I wonder if I should save her a copy.

Christopher Parkhurst, My Daughter's Husband

When Chris proposed to Tessa, he surprised her by making a special dinner, by covering the floor with rose petals, and by getting down on one knee to ask the "will you?" question. For her last birthday, he bought airline tickets to New York so she could see one of her best friends. For the holidays, he agrees to come with Tessa for a home visit. I listen to such tales for evidence, and I conclude Chris does what a good son-in-law should do: he makes my daughter happy.

Chapter 18
Stories We Do and Do No/Tell

When my parents would introduce their three children, they would say, "This is Gus, our eldest son, Ronnie, our second son, and our adopted daughter, Michele." I heard this introduction so many times that it became unremarkable to me until I mentioned to a few friends that my parents would always introduce my sister as adopted. With grace, they articulated their disapproval of such an introductory entry. Whether or not my sister felt the weight of that introduction over the years, I do not know, but perhaps it did in part motivate her to find her biological parents at the age of thirty. She decided that it would be hurtful to my parents if she told them of her desire, particularly given her deep love for them and the repeated adoption story they always tell:

> We don't know much, except that you were left by your mother with a babysitter. She never returned, and the babysitter turned you over to the adoption agency. After we learned we couldn't have any more children, we still wanted a girl, so we decided to adopt. After all the initial screening, we had the opportunity to pick out the child we wanted. There you were, in a room full of children, just two years old, sitting all by yourself, your nose running and with such a sad look on your face, we knew you were a child who needed a home. And out of all the children there, we picked you.

Michele's search was not easy. She knew my uncle was the lawyer who handled the case, but even after extended discussions with him, she learned little. She fought the courts to get her official records released from the adoption agency, a task much more difficult back then than now. When her papers were finally released, she discovered her biological mother's name and that she was not married when she left Michele behind. Armed with a name, she continued her long search, often leading to dead ends, before she found a woman in Kentucky who, without acknowledging that she was her mother, wanted the opportunity for them to meet. This began a long term relationship, one marked by evasion and silence around the question of parentage, but with enough circumstantial evidence to make my sister confident that she had found her biological mother. As the years unfolded, as the interaction with her biological mother continued, she also came to believe another thing about her parentage: her biological father was our father. Michele concluded that she was conceived as a result of our father's affair.

My parents continue to tell their adoption story while Michele, Gus, and I simply nod and smile. Their tale is a good story, one with a happy ending and one, as best as we can tell, they can live with. Perhaps it is the story they now believe to be true. I hold Michele's story against the one I read in H. L. Goodall's (2006) *A Need to Know: The Clandestine History of a CIA Family*. Michele's story is not Goodall's tale. It does not have the political implications or intrigue that Goodall's narrative does. It does not make me question the illegal actions of our government the way Goodall's book does. Yet, on a personal level both Michele and Goodall had a need to know, had a need to find a narrative that would hold still. What their stories teach me is that the reach for narrative is the stretch we take to make sense of our lives. And, as Goodall's mother might say, "It's complicated." I want in the rest of this essay to discuss that complication, to point to some of the lessons Goodall provides about the stories we do and do not tell ourselves.

Goodall first reminds us that "we are shaped by our memories and circumstances, and each and every morning we awake to carry ourselves and who we are into the world and see what happens. We make all of it up as we go along" (p. 348). How we make it all up as we go, *A Need to Know* teaches us, depends not only on the memories we hold and circumstances we live, but also on the liberties we take with what we believe are the facts of our lives and the demands those facts place upon us. Sometimes, for example, our truths are too hard to face, so we maneuver and manipulate them until we can create stories that will obscure or alter the facts, keep them from view, even from ourselves. Perhaps this was the case with Goodall's parents whose drinking and drug abuse was often left unspoken. Perhaps this accounts for my parents' adoption story. Other times when our facts become unsettled, slippery, shaken, we reach for new truths, like my sister did when she learned her adoptive father was her biological father, or like Goodall did when he realized there was much more to his mother's and father's stories than he had ever been told. And when those truths become unsettled, slippery, shaken, we search for the next truth that might offer some anchor. And there are other times when we feel we must conceal the facts of our lives—we are too ashamed, too afraid, or too accountable to share what we know. We live with our secrets, like Goodall's and my parents', sometimes in comfort and sometimes with pain. Facts are what we make them and what they make us.

Goodall also teaches us that our stories do not live in isolation; they are tested, refined, and tested again until the storied self emerges. Goodall writes, "We develop a story of the self for ourselves, one that we practice on myriad audiences, each time gauging the responses we receive from others, using those responses to make modifications on our story line" (p. 190). Through practice, we learn what stories seem true and what stories can be made to appear true. In each case, we make who we are, a storied identity that can comfortably settle or that demands retellings, modified for the tensions we may feel. Most of the time, my sister simply describes herself as adopted. Given her circumstances, Goodall's mother, Naomi May Saylor Goodall, finds the background story of her life she is compelled to tell is best rendered by simply saying she is from Virginia rather than West Virginia. For her, this small linguistic omission makes a better tale, a better self.

Goodall notes that the stories we tell are always "a version of the truth, not the whole truth, or maybe even the main truth" (p. 155). Stories, constituted in language as they are, always fall short of full representation, even when we believe we have all the facts at hand. When we have limited factual information at our disposal, our stories are built on probability, possibility, and propelling desires. Neither my sister nor Goodall knows the full story of their fathers' lives. They tell their tales with caution, reminding listeners of their speculations and hinting at their vested interests. In their need to know, they do not want their stories to do harm.

Doing no harm for Goodall and my sister means, in part, to respect those they love, despite whatever flaws they might see. Their tales are told in sympathy with those they name, in sympathy with the struggles we all face as we move through our lives. They know that families are often delicately balanced systems, constructed through carefully made scripts, and written in codes for use both within and outside their walls. Goodall notes: "Communication in any family is a complex of systemic language loops and feedback information. One word or phrase becomes intricately connected to another word or phrase in the systemic family psyche. Every family has a codebook to decipher the deeper meanings of those words" (p. 333). Goodall and my sister know when to open the codebook and when to leave it shut and, perhaps more importantly, for whom the code might be deciphered. Some codes are best left secret; some best revealed.

Our stories are acts of privileging what we deem worthy of telling, and as our tales unfold, we decide who the central characters are and how they are to be rendered. This claim, of course, is not surprising, but it stands along side Goodall's chilling reminder: "Minor characters are easily forgotten, as expendable as ex-wives or the people we once called our friends" (p. 153). My sister seldom mentions my mother when she tells her tale, seldom considers what my mother actually knew, seldom ponders what it must have meant to take Michele into her house. Goodall's story is told from his point of view, his struggle to discover his parents' hidden lives. The people that circulate around his parents' lives only matter to the extent that his parents might be understood in relationship to them. We live as minor characters in others' stories; only in our own tales do the plots center on ourselves. And in that centering, we might ask who do we diminish, deny, or delete? All stories, as Goodall knows well, carry consequences.

That is perhaps why Goodall writes, "I want you to see them [my parents] as incomplete and vulnerable persons, like all of us, made more so by the secrets they kept and by the lies they told, but good people nonetheless" (p. 295). Goodall, in his need to know, recognizes that his story matters, that there is no easy control of the sense that others might make of the stories we tell. At best, all we can do is to try to make our meanings clear, our motives apparent, our understandings generous. And we can stop, whenever possible, hiding behind our secrets. When we do so, we discover we are all "incomplete and vulnerable" people.

"A life of secrecy begins with the first secret" (p. 233), Goodall tells us. Our stories can hide or reveal. When we decide that revelation is not a plausible option, when we obscure ourselves because of legal, social, or relational laws, we commit to a hidden self whose sense of worth depends upon continued faith in the laws. We use those laws to justify our deceptive stories, to justify our actions. At times, perpetuating the secret may be the correct choice for us. It may allow us to hold much that we value in place. Other times, when we feel the foundation of those laws that support our secrecy cracking, we are likely to crack with it. Such is the case for Goodall's father whose secrets for much of his life march in concert with his allegiances and the CIA world in which he operates. But when his faith is shaken, his secrecy provides little support. My parents, on the other hand, have maintained their secret for over fifty years, believing, I imagine, that they are protecting my sister and perhaps themselves by refusing to acknowledge my father's infidelity. In doing so, they fail to realize that their hidden story, if exposed, could place them in a better light. I'm proud that my father, when he learned that my sister had been abandoned, came forward and that my mother was willing to stand beside him. Some of the secrets we keep, we keep because we cannot find the story we need to tell.

Stories, Goodall instructs, gain their weight in relationships, in how they unfold in our own and others' lives. As Goodall writes, "It is a relational truth that teaches us we are here not for a reason, not for a purpose, but for a *person*. We exist *for* them. We exist *with* them. We do not exist without them, although our bodies may continue to march on" (p. 356). More often than not, our need to know is a relational need, a need to story those in our lives in a way that settles, if only momentarily, a need that allows us to know who we are. Goodall's need to know is our need to know.

Postscript

As our father pushed his way into his nineties, Michele still had nagging doubts about her patrilineage. She decided she would only know for certain if she did a DNA test. Carefully, secretly, she captured pieces of

Dad's hair and sent them and strands of her own away for the definitive verdict. When the results were returned, she discovered that she and our dad do not share a genetic link. He is not her biological father.

"I can't believe all these years I believed he was my biological father," Michele says. "I was so sure. All the evidence suggested that he was."

"You don't think the DNA test could be wrong, do you?" I ask.

"It better not be given what I paid to have it done." I laugh and shake my head. After a moment, she continues, "It really doesn't matter. I just wanted to know for medical reasons, so I'd know and my kids would know what's in their background. Daddy is my daddy no matter what. We may not share blood but we share love."

"You can be certain of that," I reply, believing in the truth of that claim, believing that some facts will never change. "Do you think Dad had an affair?" I add.

"Maybe so. Maybe she just told Dad I was his kid. Who knows?" Michele says, sounding resigned to never knowing.

When I presented the first part of this essay at a conference, a woman who I did not know walked directly toward me immediately after the panel: "Are your parents still living?" she wanted to know.

"Yes," I said. A look of complete disgust came across her face and she turned on her heels and marched away. Her message was clear: I was unethical. I should not have revealed my parent's secret, at least not while they were living. I've used the logic that they would never know, a rationale that Ellis (2007) rightly cautions against, to justify my actions. I've taken comfort in the fact that I cleared my presentation with Michele. After all, I say, it really is her story. But most all, I've listened to Chris Poulos (2009) who convinces me that a storyteller might "evoke, emit, and open the secret lives of families into stories of powerful, transformative healing" (p. 26). Like Poulos, my wish is that this telling shows a "way to transfigure silence into talk that counts" (p. 16). I want, because it is Michele's desire, my parents to keep the story they tell. Perhaps, their story holds more truth than we thought. And I want Michele to story this tale in whatever way she needs, in whatever way she needs to know.

Chapter 79
Remains

A year after hurricane Katrina hit, my brother says, "Mom has always been a person of things. You can't separate her from her things." I nod, knowing he is right. My brother Gus and his wife Debbie had taken Mom and Dad from their home in New Orleans before the water came, before the levees broke and their city of eighty-eight years joined Lake Pontchartrain. Sitting in twelve feet of water for days, the things from the first floor of my parents' home were lost. Only the things from the second floor were saved, the place they had stopped going because of the stairs, the place where the unused and discarded were kept. In this essay I dig into the remains of my parents' material possessions after they escaped hurricane Katrina and relocated in Lake Charles, Louisiana. I search through their salvaged belongings, opening box after box and studying shelf after shelf, to consider how identity, memory, and story are linked to objects held and lost.

Learning What Was Left

When the movers arrive, their truck packed to the brim, they unload what is left, filling my parents' new two car garage. My elated mother starts digging into box after box to see what is there. "I didn't think there would be so much stuff," she exclaims. As we open boxes, a grayish-green powder attaches to our fingers, fills our nostrils. "Where did all this dirt come from? What's this smell?" Mom asks.

"I think it's mold, Mom," I answer. "Let's make sure we clean anything you want to bring in the house. Otherwise, your new house will smell like this."

"I'll get a pan of water with some soap," she says, ready to dive again into her treasures.

"Mom, I don't think breathing all this in can be good for you," I caution.

"I have to see what's here," she says firmly. I know that there is no stopping her, that stopping her would do more harm than the mold. She needs to know what is left.

So, we move through box after box, deciding what to keep, what demands a story. "Look," Mom urges, putting a picture of her mother in my hands, "That's Bobbi in her wedding dress. She was so beautiful as a young girl." The picture is a faded black and white, tinged with a red coloring in a battered wooden frame. The glass covering is cracked, two long lines plunging from the top to the bottom, one cutting across my grandmother's cheek. I wipe the glass and see her smile.

"Let's get another frame for this, Mom. This is an eachy-peachy." An "eachy-peachy" is what in my family we called possessions of special value. My dad kept his eachy-peachies in the bottom drawer of his dresser. When I was a kid, Dad would invite me to look at his eachy-peachies. Each had a story. All are now gone.

"Yes, that is an eachy-peachy," Mom concurs. I remove the picture from its frame and then toss the frame and broken glass into the second trash bin that is already becoming full. The movers, as instructed, had boxed everything they found still dry—cancelled checks from twenty years ago, old clothes that no longer fit my parents, advertisements for the Piggly Wiggly grocery stores from when my dad was working as a wholesale grocer. I start throwing things out without consulting my mom. "You're not throwing away any of my eachy-peachies, are you?" Mom inquires as I lift a box into the trash.

"No, Mom. So much of this is just garbage," I answer. She gives me a suspicious look but says nothing. "Mom, we need a strategy for getting through all this," I offer. The grime and smell is getting to me. "I'll start stacking all the boxes of books in the corner and all the Christmas decorations over there," I say pointing. "We can go through those another time."

"Okay, but see if you can find *The Robe* in the book boxes," Mom says.

"*The Robe*?" I question.

"Yes, that's my favorite book—it tells the story of what happened to the robe they wrapped Jesus in after they took him down from the cross. Have you read it?" Mom asks.

"No, Mom."

"Oh, you should. It's just wonderful."

"Mom, what would you do with it if I found it? With your eyes, you can't read any more." I say without thinking.

"I know, but I would still like to have it," she answers. I go through box after box of books, but I never find *The Robe*.

"Oh, look. Here're all my decorations from my gold Christmas," Mom cries. "I think that was my prettiest one."

"Yes, that was pretty," I agree.

"I think these three boxes contain sewing stuff, Mom," I say, carrying a box for her to see.

"Yes, those are my patterns. Don't throw those away," Mom orders. Obeying, I set the boxes aside but I wonder why she would want these old, moldy, out-of-style dress patterns, particularly given that she can not see well enough to sew.

Reading my mind, she says, "Perhaps the girls will want them." The girls refer to my wife, my brother's wife, and my sister. We have set other items aside for their consideration that I'm sure they don't want. It's a necessary step before Mom will be ready to let it go.

"Mom, here's a box filled with papers you and Dad might want. Why don't we go in for a while?" I am worried that Mom is doing much more than she should. "You can rest while I tell you what's here. You can tell me what to keep and what to toss," I offer.

Once inside, with Mom and Dad comfortable on the couch, I start sifting through the papers. "This looks like some policy from TransAmerica," I say, opening the stiff pages.

"What's the date on it?" Mom asks.

"Let me see. 1984."

"We don't need that. Throw it away," Mom says.

"It looks like there are some old tax records in here," I offer.

"Don't let him see how rich I am, Merle. He'll want to do me in," Dad chimes in.

"Dad, if I were going to do you in, I would have done it long ago when you had some money," I tease.

"If they aren't recent, just toss them," Mom says.

"What's Ronnie doing, Merle?" Dad asks.

"He's going through some of our old papers that we salvaged from the flood," Mom answers.

"What flood?"

"The flood that made us move to Lake Charles, honey," Mom replies, glancing at me, wanting me to note the state of my dad's Alzheimer's disease.

"We're in Lake Charles?"

"Yes, honey. We moved here after Katrina wiped out our home in New Orleans," Mom says, answering with patience the same question he's asked over and over again.

"I'll be damned," Dad responds, speaking in Greek.

"Here's Uncle Harry's obituary," I say, returning to the contents of the box.

"When Uncle Harry died, I became the patriarch," Dad notes, with a touch of sadness. Then, raising his finger into the air and mimicking Uncle Harry's boisterous proclamations, he adds, "It all started with the Greeks."

"I want that," Mom says.

"You do?"

"Yes, that's how you keep family history," Mom states, offering a lesson I'm invited to learn. As I continue through the box, I find little of value, except a few old photographs and more and more obituaries.

"Here's the obituary for Jimmy Evans," I say.

"He was my best golf buddy. We did a lot of great trips with Rita and Jimmy," Dad remembers, his distant memory still fully intact.

"Here's Jack McCullum's," I note.

"Jack loved his sports. He passed up that terrific job he could have had just so he could keep playing on his softball team. Olga was so mad," Dad recalls.

"The sad thing about growing as old as we have is that you lose all your friends and relations. Watching one after another go is just too hard. It's hard growing old," Mom says, providing another lesson to be learned.

I stop telling them when I find another obituary. Sharing them seems cruel, heartless. Without another word, I put the family ones in a pile to keep, and those of their friends I drop into the trash.

"I think I'm too tired to do any more today," Mom says. The next day Mom is coughing. Her eyes are watering and her nose is running.

"Mom, did all that mold get to you?" I ask, worried.

"I guess it did. I had a rough night," Mom says while blowing her nose and then adds, "I think I better take it easy today."

"Your things aren't going anywhere, Mom," I offer, hoping she doesn't want to dig into more boxes.

"There's not much out there. Not too many eachy-peachies."

"You're right, Mom, there isn't much there."

"All my good things were on the first floor," Mom says, her eyes watering, either from the mold or from the memories.

"Yeah, you had some good stuff, Mom."

"What are you and Ronnie talking about?" Dad inserts.

"Nothing, honey. Nothing."

Learning What Was Kept

Two months later I return for another visit. The garage is mostly empty and their new house fully decorated. Mom always had an exquisite decorating eye. Her house, always tastefully done, would never give a hint of her age. Years ago she decided, confident against the skepticism of her husband and her children, she wanted pink carpet for her living room. Selecting the right sofa and chairs, the right lamps, and the right accouterments, she pulled together a room that could have easily been featured in *Southern Living*. Now, her new home is filled with knick-knacks. Shelf after shelf holds items she never before would have put on display. After settling in, I ask, "Mom, what are all those things you have all around?"

"Do you think they look tacky?" she probes, watching me.

"No," I answer, hoping I wouldn't get caught in my lie.

"Well, I do, but I want to have those things out so I can see them," Mom says. "Come with me and I'll give you a tour."

She leads me into the kitchen where three glass-encased shelves hold perhaps twenty items. She opens the doors and reaches for a small teapot.

"This is the only thing I have left from my childhood tea set. When I was little, Bobbi and I would have tea parties. I would serve her and she would tell me how a lady was supposed to behave." Then, after a short pause, Mom adds, handing me the teapot, "She always loved her tea." I take it and see two painted roosters facing each other, each one, I believe, is crowing its survival. Thinking of my mother's small hands that served her mother, my large paws return the roosters to their place on the shelf.

"Those are the ceramic doves and right behind them is the porcelain vase I made," Mom says pointing. "I won first prize in the state competition for my doves and I think second or third for my vase."

"You made so many beautiful things, Mom," I say.

"That's all I have left."

"I still have the lamp you gave me," I offer.

"You do?" She asks, sounding pleased.

"Yes, it's in my study."

"I'm glad you have it," Mom says, and then a pink egg catches her eye. "I made your dad buy this for me. I have no idea why I wanted it."

"Everybody has to have an egg," I joke.

After looking at several more things on the kitchen shelves, Mom directs me to the book shelves. "You see this," Mom says, pointing to an old iron now serving as a bookend. "That was my Grandma Schaeffer's iron. She would heat it up on her wood stove to do her ironing. When your grandfather gave her an electric stove, she pushed it in the corner and refused to use it."

Mom moves to the next item on the shelf. "And this is your Great Aunt Lula's cup and saucer."

"My Great Aunt Lula?" I question, unaware I had a great aunt name Lula.

"Yes, Aunt Lula was your grandfather's sister. She died when she was eighteen. People died young in those days. I think it was her appendix."

Reaching up to the next shelf of the bookcase, Mom pulls down a small ash tray, decorated with pink roses on each side and a small matching cup. "You'd put cigarettes in there when you had company," Mom says, showing me the cup. "That was a wedding gift your dad and I got sixty-eight years ago." My mind races, imagining them at the age of twenty, sitting together, opening their wedding gifts. They come to me in a black and white photograph. I see them, my mother leaning forward, unwrapping; my father leaning back, smiling, his eyes on my mother. I am brought back to the present as my mother continues telling the stories of the items on the bookshelves. She then guides me to the mantel.

"Here's Bobbi's angel. She kept it on her coffee table for as long as I can remember," Mom shares. The angel, painted in soft pastels, stands on a pedestal playing a violin. I lean in to hear what it is playing.

"You silly thing," Mom laughs, slapping my arm. I laugh, too, but in that moment I thought perhaps that angel might be playing.

"Here. Read this," Mom orders, handing me a silver ladle. First I see an engraved "S."

"Is the 'S' for Schaeffer?" I ask.

"Yes. Turn it over." I read: "From the Friendly Bible Class of the Franklin St. Methodist Episcopal Sunday School, August 24, 1916."

"They gave that to Bobbi for her wedding day," Mom instructs. "And that," Mom continues, pointing to a red flower vase with a silver band around its neck, "Your dad gave to me when we were first married."

"Why are you boring Ronnie with all that talk about all that crap," Dad pipes in.

"It's not crap and Ronnie isn't bored," Mom responds. "He likes to hear about these things. Maybe one day he'll write it all down and put it in a book."

"I might, Mom," I say, recognizing the privilege of being taken on the tour of what was kept. "Mom, you have some wonderful things."

"I know. I know I'm lucky. So many people lost so much more than we did. But still, I can't help thinking about all that is gone— the crystal paperweight my brother Gene gave to me, Grandma Schaeffer's ink holder and Grandpa's clock, Grandma Clemens's beautiful table with the marble top, your grandfather's rocker, the one that I covered with the needlepoint rose pattern, and all the things in your dad's dresser. He had all the scrapbooks in there for all of you kids—all your achievements washed away. Dad had his wedding ring in there. That's gone, too."

"The important thing is that you and Dad got out safely," I say.

"I know but ...." Her voice trails off.

"Sounds like you and Mom are having a sad conversation," Dad inserts.

"No, Dad. We're just remembering," I respond.

"I don't like remembering things that make me sad," Dad confesses.

"Me neither, Dad." But I believe I will not forget how my mother put on display her things, things of little value except in how they connect lives, in how they help us remember what matters. My mother teaches me that we find each other in what is kept and lost. My mother knows that what is left tells the story of what is lost and what is lost tells the story of what is left. My mother sits next to my dad on the couch, holding his hand, feeling for his missing ring.

Learning What Was Next

I arrive the day after Christmas for our family celebration, wondering what traditions will be kept and what ones will be lost in our second Christmas following Katrina. Mom and Dad's house is decorated in gold, except for five small Christmas trees of varying height and color placed together on a table. This Christmas forest holds a charm, an artistic touch, an invitation for the eyes to linger. On the mantel is a nativity scene, and each table is adorned with a golden Christmas figure, dish, or wreath. Mom has insisted on hosting the family Christmas party and does her best to replicate Christmas of years past—the opening of the gag gifts, presents and checks for all her kids and grandkids, and ham as well as turkey with all the side dishes for dinner.

"Mom, you've done too much," I say, thinking of all her labor, of the cost to her health.

"I wanted it to be like it was," Mom answers.

My first thought is that it will never be like it was in the old house, but I look around the room and everyone is there. Counting the grandkids and great grandkids, eighteen of us have gathered. "I just worry that you push yourself too much," I remark.

"It's just so nice to have all you kids here," Mom says.

"Where's Blake? He couldn't make it?" Dad, referring to one of my sister's three sons, wants to know.

"He was here," Mom responds. "Remember, he had to leave early."

"He was here?" Dad questions again.

"Yes, honey, he was here," Mom repeats.

As the party winds down, my sister, Michele, and I start with the clean-up. "Don't worry about all that," Mom calls into the kitchen.

"We're just putting away all the food," Michele calls back. Then she turns to me. "Have you looked in Mom's fridge?"

"Not that I remember."

"I doubt if we'll be able to get anything in there. Same for the freezer she insisted I get for her. Both are absolutely full," Michele says.

"She always would buy for any party more food than she needed," I respond, missing Michele's point.

"It's not just that," Michele whispers. "Mom is hoarding food. She saves everything, even the smallest of leftovers. She's constantly sending me to the store to buy more. Most of the time she already has what she sends me to get. She won't throw anything away, even if it's gone bad."

I open the doors to the fridge—it is full. I can't imagine how we are going to fit what is still out on the counter. "Wow," I offer, closing the door to the fridge. "It's kind of like when Mom put that deposit on the apartment in New Orleans, signed a year long contract for that little apartment she and Dad were in while she was in middle of buying this house. She was hoarding houses."

"Right," Michele responds, glad I'm catching on.

"Have you said anything to Mom about this?" I ask.

"Yes, but she just says that since she and Dad can't drive, she has to get her supplies when she can, and I understand that. But whenever Mom invites us over for dinner, we tell her we'll do pick-up because we're scared to eat what she has in there. Then, whatever is left goes in the fridge."

Mom enters before I have chance to respond to Michele. "Mom, we were just wondering how we're going to fit all this food in your fridge," I say.

"Maybe we can put some in the freezer," Mom suggests.

"That's full, too," Michele comments.

"We'll find a way," Mom says with confidence. She turns to the fridge. "Let me do some arranging." After a moment, she's found space for the remaining ham. "I can mix these carrots with these peas—that will give us a little more space." She continues combining, stacking, balancing, and shifting her food until she gets it all put away. "There," she says triumphantly.

"Mom, I'm afraid when you open that door it will all come falling out on you," I say joking, but wondering what should be done with Michele's concern. There are things in there I doubt could any longer be call food. "Do you know what's in there?" I ask.

"Yes, I know," Mom responds, sounding a bit defensive. "Let's go sit down," Mom suggests, changing the subject.

We move into the living room and join my dad. "Where have you all been? I was lonely," Dad says, half joking, half serious.

"We were putting away the food, Dad," Michele answers.

"Did you hear what Gus told me earlier?" Mom questions. We shake our heads. "He said it would be years before we can go back to New Orleans. Nobody is rebuilding in our section, he said. He said it's like a ghost town. No grocery stores, no drug stores, no anything."

"Yeah," I say, "Gus did tell me that."

"What's worst," Michele adds, "is that you can't get medical services. If you go the emergency room, you may have to wait seven or eight hours to see a doctor."

"I want to go back home," Mom says. "I miss New Orleans."

"Mom, the New Orleans you want to go back to isn't the New Orleans that is there," I offer.

"Years, Gus said. At our age, we don't have years," Mom blurts out.

"Years before what?" Dad wants to know.

"Before we can return home," Mom says, taking Dad's hand. She rubs the wedding ring she gave him for Christmas.

"We aren't home?"

"No, darling, we're in Lake Charles."

"Lake Charles? What are we doing in Lake Charles?" Dad asks, becoming more confused with each answer Mom gives.

"We came here because of the flood?"

"What flood?

"Oh, honey, don't you remember? The flood from Katrina."

"We're not in New Orleans?" Dad questions again, struggling to make sense of what Mom is saying.

"No, darling. We're in Lake Charles. This is our home now." Michele and I exchange glances, thinking about Dad and wondering if Mom is accepting that Lake Charles is now her permanent home.

"It is? I'll be damned," Dad says in Greek, ending his questions. "Well, if this is our home, you better put me to bed, honey. But no sex tonight, woman, I'm too tired," he teases.

"Aw," Mom teases back, "I was hoping to get a little."

After the goodnights, Michele and I are left on the couch. "They're so cute together," Michele says.

"Yeah, and so sweet. Mom has the patience of a saint," I add.

Michele nods. "I think they liked what they got for Christmas."

"Yeah, more things," I respond with a small laugh. Michele laughs, too.

"Do you think we did the right thing letting them get this house? Gus thinks we should have insisted that they move into assisted living," Michele notes.

"I don't think Mom would have agreed."

"I don't either." Michele reaches for the golden glazed Santa on the coffee table. "I remember this from when I was a kid. I always found it a little creepy."

"I think Mom made it—one of her ceramic pieces," I say. Michele turns Santa over and carved on the bottom is "Merle."

"Yeah, it's Mom's."

"It won't be too many more years before you'll be putting that creepy Santa out on your coffee table," I tease.

"No, I want the red flower vase Dad gave to Mom," Michele jokes.

"It's yours," I laugh. We sit quietly for a moment considering the implications of our exchange.

"Is there anything we should be doing?" Michele asks.

"I don't know."

"I just wonder what's next," Michele says.

"Who knows what's next?"

Chapter 20
Loss

"There is no right way to do loss," a friend said to me shortly after Dad died. This piece is about one doing, one moving through the process, one handling. It comes to me on the first anniversary of Dad's death. It rushes forward in waves of insistent images, in collected and constructed tales, in needed memories. I fall into a fragmentary organization for my thoughts: waiting for the end to come, participating in rituals, disquieting and joyful rememberings, fortunate and unfortunate forgettings, putting others' claims and experiences against my own, holding on by telling, and seeing what is left behind. Such an ordering is a means of recovery, a way of sharing what inevitably comes, told with the aim of laying bare one person's experience of loss. I believe, as Bochner, Ellis, and Tillman-Healy (1997) note, "we are storytellers seeking meanings that help us cope with our circumstances. Our stories must be adequate for the situations with which we must deal" (p. 312). Here is one telling.

Waiting for the End

My wife Mimi and I were the last to arrive after my brother Gus called and said that we probably ought to come. I packed a black suit. The drive from Carbondale to Lake Charles took two days, and when we arrived, Dad had already been sent home to die. My mother had envisioned that Dad could rest on the sofa in the living room and we would all sit around and chat. "Dad would love that," she said. But when he arrived home, he came with a medical bed, was placed in his bedroom, and was railed in. He was too ill and too drugged to be any place else. We would take turns, leaving the chat of the living room and going to the quiet of the dying room. He moved in and out of consciousness. Whenever he would slip away into unconsciousness, the nurse would say, "He's resting comfortably now."

My sister Michele kept encouraging us to say what we needed to say to Dad before he died. I was at a loss—I didn't have a script. We did not have any tension between us that needed to be resolved. We did not have any unfinished business, unless one considers continuing to live in each other's life unfinished business. I did not think I needed to express my love for him—he knew. So I spoke to his still body when his eyes were open in the way we knew best. I teased him: "Come on, Dad. You need to stop being such a weenie man. Stop playing like you're sick just to get all this attention. I guess I'll have to get your 'weenie man' hat and put it on you." I'd like to think he took in those words and smiled to himself, knowing both their falsehood and the work they were trying to do.

My favorite moment came when Michele and I were at his bedside. She was trying to call him forward, to call him back to us. "Daddy, Daddy, Daddy," she repeated, drawing out each repeated "y" into a soft song. "What-y," came his reply. Michele and I laughed and, then, as if he had made his final playful tease, he returned to unconsciousness, to the place where our words seemed not to matter.

But mostly, it was waiting. The immediate family, sitting in the living room and talking about this and that, waited. Each of us would slip away into Dad's room and, when we returned, would give a short report: "He seems to be sleeping now." "The nurse said his pulse and blood pressure are still strong." "I think he recognized me." And we waited. Between the waiting, one of us would remember the business of living: "I'll go get us some sandwich-makings for lunch." "I need to walk around the block—I just can't sit any longer." "Mom, you've got to eat or you'll be sick too." But mostly, we just waited.

Living the Rituals

Dad's body was moved from Lake Charles to New Orleans for the burial. He lived in New Orleans for eighty-eight of his ninety-one years, lived and relished the pleasures of the Big Easy until Katrina hit, until Katrina buried his home under water, until Katrina washed away the place that was his anchor. Mom insisted that New Orleans is where he had to be buried and that is where she would be buried when her time came.

Before the services, Gus asked me if I thought it would be a good idea to put a golf club in the casket, and I said that it would be a beautiful touch that Dad would appreciate. Gus placed a putter and three golf balls by Dad's side. But I can imagine Dad standing by the casket, looking at the quality of putter, and saying, "I got bums for sons. Here I am on my way to heaven and this is the putter you give me to use. Bums! Merle, we've got bums for sons." And I can imagine Dad commenting on all the flowers—"how nice!" he would say, rolling the two words almost into a song. He would pause by the photo display to make sure each of his seven grandchildren was pictured and to tell stories of growing up on General Pershing Street with his father and mother and his three brothers and two sisters. He would pick up the guestbook to make sure he hadn't missed anyone who came. He would listen to the eulogies of his grandson and his son-in-law and joke, "I did all that?" but he would take in their moving words.

And, whenever he saw someone shedding tears, he would offer comfort: "I had a good life. No need for that." And I imagine Michele hearing Dad say, "No need for that," right before she rushed from the parlor. "This is barbaric," she cried, feeling the weight of inviting emotions to be present, inviting the loss in, inviting death's cold celebration. And I imagine when he saw his legally blind bride of sixty-eight years wearing one brown and one black shoe, he would say, "I'm sorry, darling, I wasn't there to help you find the right match."

The funeral home provided laminated copies of Dad's obituary for members of the immediate family. I find myself, over and over, taking it out, reading the words that identify who is left and who is not, reading the words that note he was a longtime member of the New Orleans Kiwanis Club and St. Lukes Methodist Church and that he was an avid golfer, and reading the words that tell when services will be held. As I read, I want to fill in the space between these reductive lines, want to keep him from being just a couple of column inches, want to make him a living presence. I know my added words are an incomplete gesture as they work to bring him to me. I want more. Much more. I continue to grasp the document of his death and my eyes inevitably come to rest on his small photograph. His head is cocked slightly to the side, and he holds a small smile. It is a look I know. It is as if he has just taken in what I have said and he is sizing me up, soon to offer a playful rejoinder. Or perhaps, he is just posing for the camera having become accustomed in his later years to our efforts to keep him with us, to snap him in place. But, of course, photography is no better than words.

Now, I wonder why I am writing, knowing the futility of it all, knowing the unavoidable failure.

Remembering

Dad died in August and, now, a year later, he is still coming to me. At times he arrives in the memories of others. "My favorite time with your dad," Mimi shares, "was when he and I were playing gin. We started playing two different version of the game and soon we were both accusing the other one of cheating. 'You can't do that,' he protested. 'Well, you can't do that. That's not in the rules,' I answered. We laughed and teased each other the whole game. His short term memory may have been gone, but in many ways he was sharp as a tack. After we finally got the rules straightened out, I think he beat me by more points than I care to recall."

"I feel very lucky," my cousin Lynn offers, "that he lived in Lake Charles his last few years. It gave me a chance to spend lots of time with him before he died. Richard and I would often bring over crabs or crawfish on Sunday night. We'd all just sit there chatting and picking at the seafood and have the best of time. He wasn't the best picker, but he loved his seafood."

"I miss him," Debra, his caregiver in his last years, shares. "He was such a character. Always joking. When it was time for his bath, he'd call out to your mom, 'Merle, don't let her do that to me. Merle, come save me.' And I'd tell him, 'Nobody is going hurt you.' And he'd call out again, 'Merle, you don't want another woman seeing my thing, do you? Come save me.' He was a character."

At other times, he arrives in my dreams. In one dream, a neighbor and I were cleaning up debris from a recent storm when we decided we needed something to eat. We went into town, a town I did not know, only to discover that the only place open was Kentucky Fried Chicken. As we were standing in line, I saw Dad, a few places ahead of us in the line. He was much younger, perhaps sixty, than the ninety-one years he carried into his death. "Dad," I said, "you can't be here. You're dead." "I'm just picking up a little something for your mother and me," he replied. Then he hurried off, carrying a bag of fried chicken through the deserted streets.

In another dream, Gus and I are on the beach and we are trying to bury Dad in the sand. He is lying there, his feet in the water, laughing. As we shovel the sand onto Dad, it seems to just fall way. "What are you guys trying to do?" Dad asks. "We are trying to bury you," we respond, as if all this were a big joke. "Here," Dad says, "both of you lie down." We listen and he starts shoveling. Soon, Gus and I are covered from head to foot. "That's how it is done," Dad remarks and walks off. I awake, shaking and gasping for air. I look down to see if I am still covered in sand.

At still other times, he arrives as an unexpected visitor who insists upon entry. He moves in, claims space, locates himself. During these momentary insertions, there is no shaking loose. I hear him reciting the Greek poem he learned in Sunday school. It roughly translates: "I can no longer make a living on the farm so I will go the city, get a gun, and rob people for a living." After his many recitations, he would always add, "Isn't that a hell of a thing to have kid say in front of the whole congregation?"

I remember his last golf swing. Gus had just bought a new set of clubs and invited us to take a look. Dad took Gus's driver in his hands and took a practice swing. Whether it was the slight incline in the front lawn, the weight of the club, or age having its way, Dad lost his balance and fell to the ground. We rushed to help him up as Mom scolded him: "What were you thinking, you old fool, swinging that club?" "I'm fine, Merle. I'm fine," Dad said as he found himself back on his feet. "But did you see that shot? It landed about three feet from the hole."

The old joke he would tell every night before going to bed returns again and again. "Do you know why you go to bed?" he would ask, and then wait for us to complete the form. "No, why?" we would sometimes dutifully reply, but more often we would either provide the standard answer or disrupt what we knew was to come. "To get to other side of the road," we might joke. And he would shake his head: "No, not to get to the other side of the road. You go to bed because the bed won't come to you."

Come to me, Dad. Claim as much space as you would like. I will listen to you recite yet again your Greek poem. I will help you up after your mighty last swing. I will play my part in your corny jokes. I will let you in my dreams. I will enjoy your company there. I will be ready for stories, stories that tell how you are missed. Or, let me find the words; let me come to you.

Locating Loss

I read for what resonates, for echoes to my own experience, for what provides comfort. Like any good academic, I read trying to understand. I read in the belief that others' stories will offer insight, will place death in its place, will offer some narrative closure. I read in hope. I read feeling maudlin and macabre.

Clergy, health care professionals, and scholars who work with loss are familiar with its standard stages: denial, anger, bargaining, depression, and acceptance (Kubler-Ross, 1973, 2005). The process, they suggest, takes about a year. Looking back after a year has passed, I hold myself against the expected. My one moment of denial came the night Dad died. The night nurse woke me to say that the end had come. I went to his bedside and studied his stillness. "No, he's not dead," I insisted to the nurse. "He's just sleeping."

"I'm sorry," she said. "He no longer has a pulse."

I felt for his wrist and was sure there was a small beat. "Here. Feel here."

She took his wrist. "So sorry," she repeated after a moment, "but there's nothing. He's gone."

I have felt no anger, nor have I engaged in any bargains. Perhaps if I had been in Michele's shoes and had experienced firsthand the inattentiveness and incompetence of the medical staff, I would have felt angry. But, I remain glad that Dad never knew he had cancer, that his last year was not filled with painful treatments. Perhaps if I hadn't been living for many years in what Jackson (2008) calls "anticipatory grief" (p. 277), I would have bargained for more time. I knew Dad's days, measuring beyond ninety-one years, were limited. I've felt depressed, sad, but I never allowed it to linger to what I would consider an excessive degree. I am still working on acceptance.

I read on. I have learned, despite its continued widespread use, that Kubler-Ross (2005) reconsidered her initial thinking and that other scholars have called into question the model's explanatory power. I read for order, for categories that might hold still. When no abstractions seem to provide the satisfactory summary, I read for the telling example. I read again Carolyn Ellis's (1993; 1995; 1996) moving accounts—her and Gene's story of their final years together, her brother's tragic plane-crash death, and her caregiving relationship with her mother in her mother's last years. I dig out Art Bochner's (1997) moving reflection after learning about his father's death while attending a National Communication Association Convention. I remember Leah Vande Berg and Nick Trujillo's (2009) narrative of their final days together. I recognize the pain these writers describe, the struggle, the difficult adjustment to life without a person you love. I see myself. I see us all trying to cope.

I buy Joan Didion's (2005) widely acclaimed *The Year of Magical Thinking* where she tells the story of living without her partner in the year following his death. The line from her book that haunts me comes right near the end: "I realize as I write this that I do not want to finish this account" (p. 224). It takes me to Jonathan Wyatt's writing and thinking about his father.

I first encountered Jonathan Wyatt when he was reading a convention paper about the loss of his father at the First International Conference Congress of Qualitative Inquiry in 2005. I was struck by the power of his words, was moved by the loving tribute for his father. The following year, we found ourselves in a writing workshop together. I made the point that for me writing was a way of letting go, of getting rid of what ever I was carrying. Jonathan offered alternative logic: "I write to hold on." Three years later he writes in fear that his father is slipping away:

> Does writing about my father assuage my guilt that I forget him? That my life continues without him?
>
> Does writing about him alleviate my fear? My fear of what his becoming distant, his growing absence, means?
>
> Oblivion.
>
> (Wyatt, 2008, p. 962)

I am still reading. I am still writing. Like Jonathan, I want to know that my stories "about my father [are] a way of reassuring me that they are not his last stories, that there are more to be told" (p. 962). I write to hold on.

Needing to Tell

The first time I returned to New Orleans after his death was for my nephew's wedding. My daughter Tessa and her husband Chris also came into town for the celebration. Mimi and Tessa had heard all the stories I had about Dad, but Chris was a new audience, a first timer to New Orleans and a generous listener for my need to share. "Chris, this is Decatur Street and right over there, there where that souvenir shop is now, is where Dad's business was. He was a wholesale grocer—the Jackson Wholesale Grocery. It was directly across the street from what was once the Jackson Brewery. As a kid, I worked down here—putting stamps on packs of cigarettes, making deliveries in the Quarter, putting up orders. The tobacco end of the business was run out of this narrow, maybe fifteen feet wide and 300 feet long, building. It was quite an operation. My dad always loved the Vieux Carre, from the good food to the local characters. After years of being in cramped space, my dad and his brothers moved the business to a bigger warehouse." We would walk another block and I would start again: "Over there, Dad once…"

I want everyone to know, Chris included, that Dad was a good father, convince all who do not know that my claim is based in fact. So I offer details as proof: (1) When Gus, Michele and I were little and misbehaving, he would ask, "Do I have to take this belt off?" He would make a big show of putting his hands on his belt buckle, but we all knew the belt would never come off. (2) In the summer of my seventeenth year, I wrecked the family car. No one was hurt, and the car was in good enough shape for me to get it back home. I decided I would wait until morning to tell my parents. When I awoke the next day, I went outside to once again survey the damage before facing my parents. Taped to the smashed fender was a sign in my dad's careful print: "The work of your evil twin." I went back inside and explained what my evil twin had done the night before. Dad's only comment after my explanation: "Well, we'll have to get that fixed." (3) He had mounted on velvet and framed the name plates from the trophies I had won as a junior golfer. (4) Dad made a comfortable living, but he was by no means wealthy. I graduated with three degrees without a penny of debt. (5) No matter how long a visit I would make, when it was time for me to leave, Dad would always say: "I understand that you have to get back home, but I wish you could stay longer." I'll stop my listing, not because I do not have further evidence, but because I fear the excessive, fear that my case becomes too obvious, fear that these details fail to capture his accepting and loving presence.

Dad would always sit at the head of the dining room table. It was his place, his place for telling the stories we had all heard many times, his place for reciting the Greek he remembered from his childhood, his place for eating his meals and taking his pills. When he died, I had to sit in his chair to keep from seeing where he wasn't.

And there is much I want to tell him, little things, unimportant things, but things I know he would have loved to hear. I read, for example, a survey about the American golfer in *Golf Magazine* (Barrett, C., 2009). One of the questions was would you rather "play a round with Tiger Woods or 'play around' with Angelina Jolie?" 82 percent of the golfers surveyed before the scandal picked Tiger (p. 93). Who knows what the numbers might be now. But Dad would have loved that. He, too, would have picked Tiger.

Forgetting

Golf was our shared father/son activity. We spent hours together knocking that little ball around, hours together watching the pros play, hours together talking about the game. I can't remember, however, the last time we played together.

Each morning and evening of his last years were filled with taking pills. Slowly, painfully, he would ingest one after another. My mother would say, "Come on, honey, get your pills down," and he would take one. Then, he would forget the task at hand until her next urging. I would sit there watching, waiting for all the pills to be taken in. I can see them, spread out in front of him by his orange juice, ready to be consumed. Try as I might, though, I can't recall just how many—some number that once carried such importance—pills he needed to swallow.

Each Sunday when I would call home, Dad would ask the same questions. "How are you doing?"

"Doing great, Dad."

"Good. How's Mimi?"

"She's doing fine."

"That's great. How's Tessa?"

"Great, Dad."

"Have you heard from Doug?" his questioning would end, reminding me of my estranged son.

"I only hear from him when he needs money or is in trouble," I report.

"That's not right."

"I know, Dad," I say, letting his inquiry serve as my should. He never forgot Doug, and he never let me forget.

Each day of his last years was filled with increasing forgetfulness and disorientation. "What are you doing here?" Dad would ask.

"I came to visit. I wanted to see how the old man was doing." I'd answer.

"How long have you been here?"

"About three days, Dad."

"Really?"

"Don't you remember that Ronnie took you to the doctor's yesterday?" Mom inserted.

"He did? And am I still kicking?"

"From all indications, you're still kicking, Dad," I said.

"I glad to know that." And I was glad to provide the news. Five minutes later, Dad's questions would return: "What are you doing here?"

Mom would quickly jump in. "You just asked Ronnie that."

"I did?"

"Yes, honey, you did."

'It's terrible getting old. You can't remember a damn thing," he'd say to me. I'd nod, thinking how I didn't want to forget.

The older Dad became, the more he spoke Greek and more he wanted all those around to learn it. The few words and phrases I once knew are slipping away; but, I hang on to the Greek for, "I love you very much," a phrase he would say over and over to my mother. "You know what that means?" Dad would ask Mom.

"Yes, I do," Mom would answer every time, and then repeat the phrase back to him.

Leaving Behind

Dad's clothes still hang in his closet. Whenever I would visit Mom after Dad died, she would ask if I wanted any of Dad's things. "Go look," she would say. "He had some nice clothes, some that he never got around to wearing. They're brand new."

"Mom, I don't think any of Dad's things would fit," I would answer. My reply was always both the truth and an excuse. I was almost twice my Dad's size, but what kept me from seeing if anything might fit was that I just would not feel right wearing his clothes. Perhaps it was because it would bring him too close or would bring death too near. Or perhaps it was a refusal to accept that they were no longer needed.

"Where are Dad's 'weenie man' hats?" I asked. I had given Dad for the last two Christmases of his life two baseball caps, one engraved with "Weenie Man" and the other with "Super Weenie Man." Weenie man was a versatile and playful term we used in various contexts—it could be used when either of us left a putt short, when either of us was not acting like a "real man," when either us complained we couldn't do what we once could. And as Dad grew older, I found myself using "weenie man" with greater and greater frequency.

"His hats should be in there?" Mom said, but when I looked, they were no where to be found. I can remember him wearing them. "Get me my weenie man hat, Merle. I don't think I can make it out to dinner with everyone tonight," he would say. As I write this, I feel as if I am wearing one, the super weenie man one. I am the super weenie man who wants to see you wearing your hat again.

What I have instead is Dad's collection of writings. I first became aware of Dad's book when I was an undergraduate student in college. He pulled it from the shelf in his office. "This is my book," Dad said. "It's filled with great sayings." He positioned it so that I could see. It seemed that for years he had been collecting witticisms, puns, prayers, jokes, anecdotes, words of advice, and literary quotes. Only about half acknowledged its author; none had full citation. Each entry was inscribed carefully in his own handwriting, a perfect print that he could produce as quickly as anyone might create cursive. Then, flipping through the pages, he began to read, adding his own commentary: "Listen to this: 'Fat chance and slim chance mean the same thing.' This is great stuff, man. 'Change is inevitable, except from a vending machine.' Oh, I forgot. You're a college man. You need something a bit more profound. 'If you are patient in one moment of anger, you will escape a hundred days of sorrow.' That's a Chinese proverb. Good stuff, man. Here's another saying worthy of a college man: 'Knowledge is the antidote to fear.' Emerson said that."

"When you die," I blurt out, "this is what I want, Dad." I can't recall how Dad answered. My next memory of the book comes years later, after Dad retired. On a visit home, I discover that my mother has typed Dad's book. Each entry has been placed in a category; each now devoid of his careful hand. His original pages are spread out around the computer in disarray. "Oh no," I cried, "You've ruined Dad's book."

"I wanted to type it up so all the kids could have a copy," Mom says.

"That's great, Mom, but it's the original, in Dad's own hand, that is valuable."

"Really? I thought you'd like it all typed, all organized."

"That's nice, Mom, but I wanted Dad's original," I say, feeling badly I diminished Mom's efforts but feeling worse believing Dad's book was gone, beyond repair. Years later Mom has reassembled Dad's pages, each page carefully reinforced to hold it firmly in the three ringed binder. "Here, honey," Mom says, "this is for you. I know you wanted it."

"Oh, wow, Mom. Thanks," I say, my joy more than evident. Now I flip through the binder, reading words in search of my father. I do and do not find him there. As I turn a page deep into his manuscript, I discover a yellow post-it, with writing in my own hand. I do not remember the context for my words. I cannot recall the occasion. I know I did not place it there. But, I am in Dad's book. I wrote on that yellow note: "About all we can do is to keep on trying. Love, Ron." I am trying, Dad. I am trying.

Mom and Dad had two small, padded rocking chairs that were placed directly in front of the television. Placed there, Dad could hear and Mom see enough to be content. They would sit together, holding hands, gently rocking, resting their feet on two small foot stools in front of them. Several months after Dad died, I was visiting home and I found myself sitting in Dad's rocker; Mom was in hers. Her arm was resting on the arm of her rocker. I let my hand slip into hers. We sat there in silence, holding hands, watching the History Channel together. It felt oddly intimate—I hadn't held my mom's hand for any length of time since I was a child—yet, somehow, it seemed like the right thing to do.

Afterword
Leaning Toward a Way of Being

Standing as a witness to my own effort, I lean in to gather lessons that might be learned.

I have been languaging relationships, searching for words that might give the feel of experience. I've written from the heart on behalf of the heart. I've called upon the poetic to help in my task, to help me feel I pushed language as far as I could. I've looked to language for answers; I've looked to language answers. I've asked language to do considerable work even though I recognize that there is always slippage, a falling away. I've always returned, however, to language's salty promise, knowing that it is my best hope. It lets me lean in, lets me tilt in the direction of others.

I have been listening to myself and others, wanting to gather what I can, to enter a space that can be shared, to invite and to be invited. I've paused and poked, contemplated and considered, felt and fashioned a response. I've been living in the quest for understanding and carrying the realization of its impossibility. I've insisted that at least I might move closer, might find a forgiving consent, might lean in far enough that I would sense I'd done the best I could. Leaning in, I stand as reflexivity's collaborator and as empathy's champion.

I have been watching men, working to be a better one than I have been. I've believed that by naming and considering, change is possible. I've understood how habits can halt progress and how hubris can hinder growth. I've tried to heed the horrific without sacrificing the healthy. Saturated with power, men, I've come to see, need to be stripped, to stand naked, exposed. When I lean in, I can do some undressing. I find I am not helpless; I am more than culture's heir. Healing is possible. I must hurry.

I have been holding friends and lovers, trying to chronicle what counts. I've remembered friends and lovers from across a life span. I've imagined what friends and lovers might be. I've tried, by recalling and imagining drinks that would tap another's glass and beds that would hold for better or worse two embracing bodies, to offer the poem of connection. I've envisioned the pleasurable and the painful, the freeing and frozen, the tender and the tense. I lean away from the painful, frozen and tense; I lean into the pleasurable, freeing, and tender. Sometimes, against my predilections, I lean forward in the name of care. Sometimes, because I cannot do it alone, I lean on others. Sometimes, when I am at my best, I lean in with love.

I have been carrying my family, happily, sharing how one family, built on a foundation of care, might materialize. I've shaken the family tree to show how stories bind and educate, how they become a part of us. I've told of lives coming and going and I've written wanting to carry those who are gone just a little longer. I've recalled moments that I do not want to forget; I've forgotten moments I do not want to remember. I've tried, by leaning in, to do my family justice, to tell tales that they would applaud. Simultaneously, I've wanted to speak with honesty, knowing that I can only muster the honesty my love might permit. I lean in, always knowing how fortunate I am, always glad that I am there.

And as I've been languaging, listening, watching, holding, and carrying others, I've also been leaning toward you. I've liked imagining us sitting together, perhaps on a park bench on a sunny spring afternoon. You have been kind enough to lean in, to listen to my extended turn. Now I turn to you, bend forward, and say: "Tell me your stories. Share with me the poetry that makes your life speak. Do not be afraid. I will do my best to honor what you say. We are all flawed, human. Show me how we might connect." Then, you begin and I lean further in.

Standing as a witness to my own effort, I like myself best when I am struggling to find the right words, struggling to make sense of the complexity of it all; when I am listening, attentive to my own ways of being and to others; when I am watching myself, keeping myself from enacting unreflective and unproductive scripts; when I am holding with great care those I love; and when I am carrying the joyous and sorrowful lessons of family. I like myself best when I am leaning in.

Leaning

We sit, side by side, leaning in,
learning through thin whispers
why hands join and hearts explode.

We carry the load and we are made whole
by the burden and bliss of it all,
by how the telling becomes the told.

References

Alexander, B. K. (2000). *Skin Flint (Or, The Garbage Man's Kid):* A generative autobiographical performance based on Tami Spry's *Tattoo Stories. Text and Performance Quarterly* 28, 97–114.

Altman, I. & Taylor, D. A. (1973). *Social penetration: The development of interpersonal relationships.* New York: Holt, Rinehart & Winston.

Barrett, C., Ed.. (2009). 2009 Survey of the American golfer. *Golf Magazine* 51, 83–93.

Barrett, H. (2009). Maintaining the self in communication. In J. Stewart (Ed.), *Bridges not walls: A book about interpersonal communication*, 10th ed. (pp. 91–105). New York: McGraw-Hill.

Barthes, R. (1975). *The pleasure of the text.* Trans. R. Miller. New York: Farrar, Straus and Giroux.

Baxter, L. A. (1987). Symbols of relationship identity in relationship cultures. *Journal of Social and Personal Relationships* 4, 261–280.

Berg, L. V. & Trujillo, N. (2009). Cancer and death: A love story in many voices. *Qualitative Inquiry* 15, 641–658.

Berger, C. R. & Calabrese, R, J. (1975). Some exploration in initial interaction and beyond: Toward a developmental theory of interpersonal communication. *Human Communication Research* 1, 99–112.

Berger, C. R. & Kellermann, K. (1994). Acquiring social information. In J. A. Daly & J. M. Wellmann (Eds.), *Strategic interpersonal communication* (pp. 1–31). Hillsdale, NJ: Erlbaum.

Bochner, A. (1997). It's about time: Narrative and the divided self. *Qualitative Inquiry* 3, 418–438.

Bochner, A. P., Ellis, C. & Tillman-Healy, L. M. (1997). Relationships as stories. In S. Duck (Ed.), *Handbook of personal relationships: Theory, research, and interventions* (pp. 307–324). New York: John Wiley & Sons.

Butler, J. (1990). *Gender trouble: Feminism and the subversion of identity.* New York: Routledge.

Chödrön, P. (2001). *The places that scare you: A guide to fearlessness in difficult times.* New York: Shambhala.

Conquergood, D. (2002). Lethal theatre: Performance, punishment, and the death penalty. *Theatre Journal 54,* 339–367.

Cupach, W. R. (1994). Social predicaments. In W. R. Cupach & B. H. Spitzberg (Eds.), *The dark side of interpersonal communication* (pp. 159–180). Hillsdale, NJ: Lawrence Erlbaum.

Daly, J. A., Diesel, C. A., & Weber, D. (1994). Conversational dilemmas. In W. R. Cupach & B. H. Spitzberg (Eds.), *The dark side of interpersonal communication* (pp. 127–158). Hillsdale, NJ: Lawrence Erlbaum.

Didion, J. (2005). *The year of magical thinking.* New York: Alfred A. Knopf.

Doyle, J. A. (1995). *The male experience* (3rd ed.). Dubuque, IA: William C. Brown.

Dunn, S. (1994). *New and selected poems 1974–1994.* New York: W. W. Norton.

Dunn, S. (1996). *Loosestrife.* New York: W. W. Norton.

Dunn, S. (2000). *Different hours.* New York: W. W. Norton.

Dunn, S. (2003). *Local visitations.* New York: W. W. Norton.

Dunn, S. (2004). *The insistence of beauty.* New York: W. W. Norton.

Dunn, S. (2006). *Everything else in the world.* New York: W. W. Norton.

Dunn, S. (2009). *What goes on: Selected and new poems 1995–2009.* New York: W. W. Norton.

Ellis, C. (1993). 'There are survivors': Telling a story of sudden death. *Sociological Quarterly 34,* 711–730.

Ellis, C. (1995). *Final negotiations: A story of love, loss, and chronic illness.* Philadelphia: Temple University Press.

Ellis, C. (1996). Maternal connections. In C. Ellis & A, Bochner (Eds.), *Composing ethnography: Alternative forms of qualitative writing* (pp. 240–243). Walnut Creek, CA: AltaMira.

Ellis, C. (2007). Telling secrets, revealing lives: Relational ethics in research with intimate others. *Qualitative Inquiry, 13,* 3–19.

Festinger, L. (1957). *A theory of cognitive dissonance.* Stanford, CA: Stanford University Press.

Fischer, H. (March 25, 2009). United States military casualty statistics: Operation Iraqi Freedom and Operation Enduring Freedom. Congressional Research Service Report for Congress, 7-5700. Retrieved at http://www.crs.fas.org/sgp/crs/natsec/RS 22452.pdf, March 10, 2010.

Fiske, J. & Dawson, R. (1996). Audiencing violence: Watching homeless men watch *Die Hard*. In J. Hay, L. Grossberg, and E. Wartella, (Eds.) *The Audience and Its Landscape*. (pp. 297–316). Boulder, CO: Westview Press.

Fuoss, K. W. (1999). Lynching performances, theatres of violence. *Text and Performance Quarterly* 19, 1–37.

Garfinkel, H. (1967). *Studies in Ethnomethodology*. Englewood Cliffs, NJ: Prentice-Hall.

Goffman, E. (1971). *Relations in public*. New York: Basic Books.

Goodall, H. L. (2006). *A need to know: The clandestine history of a CIA family*. Walnut Creek, CA: Left Coast.

Guilmartin, N. (2002). *Healing conversations: What to say when you don't know what to say*. San Francisco: Jossey-Bass.

Heaton, D. W. (1998). Twenty fragments: The 'other' gazing back or touring Juanita. *Text and Performance Quarterly* 18, 248–61.

Heider, F. (1958). *The psychology of interpersonal relations*. New York: Riley.

Jackson, L. D. (2008). Reflections on obstacles and opportunities: Suggestions for improving the retention of female faculty. *Women's Studies in Communication* 31, 226–232, 277–286

Knapp, M. L & Vangelisti, A. L. (2005). Stages of relationships. In *Interpersonal Communication and Human Relationships*, 5th ed. (pp. 36–49). Boston: Allyn & Bacon.

Kubler-Ross, E. (1973). *On death and dying*. New York: Routledge.

Kubler-Ross, E. (2005). *On grief and grieving: Finding the meaning of grief through the five stages of loss*. New York: Simon & Schuster.

McLaughlin, M. L., & Cody, M. J. (1982). Awkward silences: Behavioral antecedents and consequences of conversational lapse. *Human Communication Research, 8*, 299–316.

Miller, R. S. (1992). The nature and severity of self-reported embarrassing circumstances. *Personality and Social Psychology Bulletin, 18*, 190–198.

Pearce, W. B. & Cronen, V. E. (1980). *Communication, action and meaning: The creation of social realities*. New York: Praeger.

Poulos, C. N. (2009). *Accidental ethnography: An inquiry into family secrecy*. Walnut Creek, CA.: Left Coast.

Rawlins, W. K. (1992). *Friendship matters: Communication, dialectics, and the life course*. Hawthorne, NY: Aldine de Gruyter.

Rawlins, W. K. (2009). *The compass of friendship: Narrative identities, and dialogue*. Los Angeles: Sage.

Richardson, L. (1997). *Fields of play: Constructing an academic life*. New Brunswick, NJ: Rutgers University Press.

Richardson, L. (1999). Feathers in our cap. *Journal of Contemporary Ethnography* 28, 660–68.

Richardson, L. (2000a). My left hand: Socialization and the interrupted life. *Qualitative Inquiry 6*, 467–73.

Richardson, L. (2000b). Writing: A method of inquiry. In N. K. Denzin and Y. S. Lincoln (Eds.), *Handbook of Qualitative Research* (2nd ed., pp. 923–948). Thousand Oaks, CA: Sage.

Rogers, C. R. (1961). *On becoming a person*. Boston: Houghton Mifflin.

Rogers, C. R. (1970). *Encounter groups*. New York: Harper & Row.

Ronai, C. R. (1995). Multiple reflections of child sex abuse: An argument for a layered account. *Journal of Contemporary Ethnography* 23, 395–425.

Russell, L. (2009). Learning to walk. *International Review of Qualitative Research* 1, 583–602.

Sanders, E. (1976). *Investigative poetry*. San Francisco: City Lights Books.

Satir, V. (1988). *The new peoplemaking*. Mountain View, CA: Science and Behavior Books.

Singer, T., B. Seymour, J. P. O'Doherty, K. E. Stephan, R. J. Dolan, and C. D. Frith. (January 26, 2006). Empathic neural responses are modulated by the perceived fairness of others. *Nature*, 466–469.

Smith, R. E. (1998). A personal look at personal narratives. In S. J. Dailey (Ed.), *The future of performance studies: Visions and revisions* (pp. 237–239). Annandale, VA: National Communication Association.

Sontag, S. (1961, 1966). *Against interpretation*. New York: Farrar, Straus and Giroux.

Stamp, G. H., Vangelisti, A. L., & Daly, J. A. (1992). The creation of defensiveness in social interaction. *Communication Quarterly, 40 (2)*, 177–190.

Stanislavski, C. S. (1924) *My life in art*. J. J. Robbins, Trans. Boston: Little, Brown.

Stanislavski, C. S. (1936). *An actor prepares*. E. R. Hapgood, Trans. New York: Theatre Arts.

Stewart, J., Ed. (2009). *Bridges not walls: A book about interpersonal communication*, 10th ed. New York: McGraw-Hill.

Tillmann-Healy, L. M. (2001). *Between gay and straight: Understanding friendship across sexual orientation*. Walnut Creek, CA.: AltaMira Press.

Tillmann-Healy, L. M. (2003). Friendship as method. *Qualitative Inquiry 9*, 729–749.

Weiner, B. (1986). *An attributional theory of motivation and emotion.* New York: Springer-Verlag.

Wood, J. (2000). *Relational communication* (2nd ed.). Belmont, CA: Wadsworth.

Wood, J. T. (2001). *Gendered lives: Communication, gender, and culture* (4th ed.). Belmont, CA: Wadsworth.

Wyatt, J. (2005). The telling of a tale: A reading of "A Gentle Going?" Paper delivered at the First International Conference Congress of Qualitative Inquiry, University of Illinois at Urbana-Champaign, IL.

Wyatt, J. (2008). No longer loss: Autoethnographic stammering. *Qualitative Inquiry* 14, 955–967.

Index

About the Author

Ronald J. Pelias is a professor and the director of graduate studies in the Department of Speech Communication at Southern Illinois University, Carbondale. He teaches in the areas of interpersonal communication, performance studies, and qualitative methods. He has placed numerous poems in such journals as *Passages North*, *Negative Capability*, *Midwest Poetry Review*, *Whetstone*, *Margie*, and *The Broome Review*, has published numerous articles and book chapters, and has directed over thirty productions for the stage. His most recent books include *Writing Performance: Poeticizing the Researcher's Body* (Southern Illinois University Press, 1999), *A Methodology of the Heart: Evoking Academic and Daily Life* (AltaMira, 2004), and with Tracy Stephenson Shaffer, *Performance Studies: The Interpretation of Aesthetic Texts*, 2nd ed. (Kendall/Hunt, 2007).